The Landscape of HOME

ALSO FROM

ROCKY MOUNTAIN  LAND LIBRARY

Home Land: Ranching and a West That Works

The
Landscape
of
HOME

A Rocky Mountain Land Series Reader

Edited by
Jeff Lee

with
John Calderazzo
SueEllen Campbell
David Waag

Illustrations by Evan Cantor

BOWER
HOUSE

DENVER

The Landscape of Home: a Rocky Mountain Land Series Reader. Copyright © 2018, 2006 by the Rocky Mountain Land Library. All rights reserved. Printed in the United States of America. No part of this book may be used or reproduced in any manner whatsoever without written permission except in the case of brief quotations embodied in critical articles and reviews. Bower House books may be purchased with bulk discounts for educational, business, or sales promotional use. For information, contact Bower House P.O. Box 7459 Denver, CO 80207 or visit BowerHouseBooks.com.

Cover design by Margaret McCullough
Text design and composition by Polly Christensen

Library of Congress Cataloging-in-Publication Data
The landscape of home: a Rocky Mountain land series reader / edited by Jeff Lee with John Calderazzo, SueEllen Campbell, David Waag.
p. cm.
Includes bibliographical references.
ISBN 978-1-917895-04-0
1.Land use—West (U.S.) 2.Land use, Rural—West (U.S.) 3.Natural resources—West
(U.S.)—Management. I. Lee, Jeff.
hd209.l36 2006
333.73'13'0978—dc22   2006024122

To Ann Zwinger

Whose spirited and constant friendship
with the Rocky Mountain West
has provided a voice for the natural world,
a model for so many writers and artists,
and inspiration for us all.

Contents

Foreword

The most important fact about Spaceship Earth: an Instruction book didn't come with it.
   — R. Buckminster Fuller

On Spaceship Earth there are no passengers; everybody is a member of the crew. We have moved into an age in which everybody's activities affect everybody else.
   — Marshall McLuhan

Hence the Rocky Mountain Land Library, which houses the collected wisdom of those devoted to the research, love and use of the land—planet Earth's gift to its inhabitants.

Along with a collection of over 15,000 volumes, the Rocky Mountain Land Library has established several outreach programs including the Rocky Mountain Land Series, an accustomed part of the Tattered Cover Book Store's monthly schedule of events. Now in its fifth year, this unique author series provides Denver audiences ready access to the authors and ideas that might eventually lead some of us to write our own instruction book, one tempered by science, poetry, history—and, as with any good instruction manual, a measure of caution and humility.

Now, in partnership with Johnson Books, the Rocky Mountain Land Library is embarking on another venture—the launch of a new series of books on the land and communities of the American West.

Just as community bookstores offer a safe haven and gathering place to explore the vastness of the ideas contained therein, the Rocky Mountain Land Library provides a valuable historical focus on matters that concern the crew of Spaceship Earth I as we work together to make a proper and safe place for future generations.

— Joyce Meskis
Owner, Tattered Cover Book Store

Acknowledgments

This anthology would not have come together if it were not for the generosity of authors, publishers, and *The Landscape of Home* editorial staff. Their donated work allows all royalties to benefit the Rocky Mountain Land Library's goal of establishing a land-study center for the Rockies. Special thanks also goes to Evan Cantor for his striking landscape images, the perfect companion for this place-based book.

We would also like to take this opportunity to thank the more than 200 authors who have generously shared their work over the course of the Rocky Mountain Land Series' first five years. And clearly, the series would have quickly foundered were it not for our faithful audience of curious readers.

Lastly, our deepest gratitude goes to the Tattered Cover Book Store and its remarkable staff for their passion and for their creation of a thoughtful venue for the exchange of ideas.

Introduction

The greatest ownership of all is to look around and understand.
—William Stafford

IT'S AN EXPERIENCE WE ALL SHARE—little by little, we wake to the world around us. As toddlers, we take a brave tumble through the grass, all senses flared. Gradually, as we grow older, we piece together a personal atlas of plants, animals, rocks, clouds, and those always shifting stars. And what becomes familiar eventually feels like home—a place we care about.

In October 2001, to advance such an intimate knowledge of our ties to the natural world, the Rocky Mountain Land Library, in partnership with Denver's Tattered Cover Book Store, established the Rocky Mountain Land Series. In its first five years the Land Series has presented over 200 author talks and workshops on topics as spirited as water in the West, wolf reintroduction, mining history, green architecture, and the power and persistence of Native American sacred sites. We've had programs on ranching history and heritage, and we've had programs on the anti-grazing movement in the West. With this series, our preeminent hope is to keep the conversation on the land alive, creating a welcoming forum for both readers and writers to come together in a spirit of honest exploration.

This book, *The Landscape of Home,* marks the 5th Anniversary of the Rocky Mountain Land Series. Within these pages, you will find eye-opening stories of the land that we hope will fire your own journey toward understanding. In *The Writing Life,* Annie Dillard asks, "Why are we reading, if not in the hope of beauty laid bare, life heightened and its deepest mystery probed?" She concludes that "We still and always want waking."

May you all wake to the words gathered here, and may you wake to the many wonders that underlie your own landscape of home.

— Jeff Lee
Director, Rocky Mountain Land Library

1 ❧ Revisiting Western Roots

Cowboys, Indians, schoolmarms, tough silences and hearts of gold: thanks to Hollywood and dime novels, people all over the world know these mythic tales of the European-American settlement of the American West. "Mythic" is the key word, of course, for these stories are not just larger and simpler than life, they are also inaccurate, both as history and—even more clearly—as outlines of the real West of today: the actual ways we live, work, and play in this vast, demanding, and beautiful land. Because the voices in The Landscape of Home *offer replacements for these familiar myths, this first section features an explanation of their genesis.*

The Wild West Masquerade

Stewart L. Udall
from *The Forgotten Founders:
Rethinking the History of the Old West*

*Stewart Udall restores to prominence the true pioneers of the westward
expansion. In "The Wild West Masquerade," he describes the mythmaking of early traveling shows, fiction, and Hollywood movies.*

For more than a century, writers, artists, and film writers fash-
ioned a mishmash of myths that came together in the form of
the Wild West, an image implanted in modern memory as the
exciting story of American westering. Overwhelmed by the legends of
these mythmakers, the settling of the Old West slouched into history
as a dramatic story of Indians attacking wagon trains and heroic U.S.
cavalrymen coming to the rescue, excited gold rushers and gunsling-
ing outlaws, and fearless sheriffs bringing order to lawless towns.

The Wild West avalanche began in 1883 when William Cody, a
consummate showman who called himself Buffalo Bill, mounted a
cowboys-and-Indians road show that lasted for three decades and
drew huge audiences in the American East and in Europe. The pageants Cody presented were so simple and dramatic that they became
the prism through which millions of Americans viewed this receding
chapter of their history.

Born in 1846, Cody spent his boyhood on a farm in Iowa during
the period when the treks of the wagon pioneers were cresting. Cody's
theatrical career as a western Everyman was launched in 1869 when
Edward Z. C. Judson, a greenhorn pulp-fiction writer who used the
pseudonym Ned Buntline, encountered him in Nebraska, listened to
his braggadocio, and wrote "Buffalo Bill, The King of Border Men"
for a New York magazine.

Attired in flamboyant frontier costumes, Cody drifted east to convert his celebrity status into cash. His colorful tales and his talents

as a thespian attracted backers. They helped him craft melodramas for New York audiences based on his purported exploits as an Indian fighter. Encouraged by what he learned in the theatrical world, on returning to Nebraska Cody staged cow boys-and-Indians pageants for local celebrations. These were so successful that he thought a touring company would be a hit in eastern cities.

Using the same techniques that made P. T. Barnum the master impresario of the nineteenth century, Bill Cody acquired investors, and in the summer of 1883 he reserved a special train and put his first Wild West show on the road. Advertised on gaudy posters as "America's National Entertainment," his vaudeville acts drew huge crowds in open-air arenas.

The performances featured tableaus of horsemanship, glimpses of native cultures, and a shooting exhibition that made markswoman Annie Oakley a household name. The finale, head lined as a scene in which "Howling Savages Pursue a Defenseless Stage Coach," was a mock battle in which an attack of blood thirsty Indians was thwarted by rough-riding cowboys armed with six-guns.

As an impresario, Cody excelled as a casting director. Some of the Indians he recruited had participated in the famous fight with Custer, and he insisted they carry their weapons and don their warbonnets. To demonstrate that the savages truly had been subdued, in 1885 Buffalo Bill hired Sitting Bull to join his tour in full regalia. The legendary Sioux war chief rode in the parades on a beautiful gray horse and held court in a tipi, where he signed autographs for awestruck visitors.

As a promoter, "Colonel" Cody did not miss a trick. To burnish his fame, he hired a ghostwriter, who produced a flow of 121 "Buffalo Bill novels" that kept him in the limelight as a symbol of the fading frontier. His popularity and profits inspired imitation, and at one point more than fifty competing traveling shows were crisscrossing the country. By changing his scenarios, Cody kept his circus like variety shows on the road for more than three decades. His pageants instilled a simple, vivid message: the West was a region where violence was an everyday experience, where hostile savages resisted the advance of pioneers, where guns prevailed over arrows and spears, and where the empire of the United States of America was enlarged by the feats of fearless cavalrymen.

With an assist from Owen Wister and Zane Grey, two extremely popular eastern novelists, by the time Cody's last show closed in

1917 his theatrical extravaganzas were accepted as the true story of western settlement. As historian Anne M. Butler reminds us, Bill Cody became "the national caretaker for western authenticity [and] almost single-handedly pushed [his] western notions into the modern scenario and made them accessible to the general public."

The whites-versus-Indians battles staged by Buffalo Bill involved fights between faceless groups. The novels of Wister and Grey provided a face—a gunfighting, justice-seeking cowboy—and a simple plot that evolved into the western, the twentieth century's most successful film formula. Moviemakers subsequently molded their protagonist into a heroic figure whose deeds made it possible to bring civilization into the American West.

Wister was a Philadelphia lawyer who spent a few summers on Wyoming ranches in the closing days of the frontier era. Grey, a young dentist from upstate New York, was so enchanted when he first saw the West in 1905 that he moved there. He became the most widely read author of his generation—15 mil lion copies of his cowboy romances were purchased by avid readers. The works of Wister and Grey made meager contributions to American literature, but the scenarios in the fictions became cornerstones of the emerging edifice known as the Wild West.

As literary heirs of the Buffalo Bill tradition, Wister and Grey exhibited little interest in the experiences of actual settlers. The quiet struggles of men and women building homes, farms, and communities in frontier settings did not appeal to their imaginations. Needing exciting action to sell their books, they portrayed the West as a male bastion of badmen, skulking Indians, and fearless cowboys whose guns protected the lives and property of their neighbors.

Wild West stories and characters were made to order for the entrepreneurs who flocked to Hollywood to develop moving pictures that would appeal to mass audiences. Scenarios featuring cowboys, horses, and guns were a natural for the first generation of filmmakers. Thus, it was no accident that Hollywood's first identifiable star would be William S. Hart, a stern, taciturn, straight-shooting cowboy. The theatrical sons of Bill Hart—progeny running a gamut from director John Ford to actor Clint Eastwood—created a genre that became a distinctive feature of American culture. Their gaudy images captured a masquerade of legends that obscured the real West.

A raft of fascinating questions is raised by the psychological process by which this new form of entertainment produced such a result. How, for example, did fictions presented to mass audiences win acceptance as capsules of actual history? Why did westerns, with their stereotyped plots and foreseeable endings, mesmerize Americans for decades? Did myths about western settlement eclipse facts in viewers' minds because the virtues and moral triumphs of the cowboy heroes were so satisfying? Or did other influences, such as the West's stunning landscapes, combine to infiltrate Wild West values and themes into the main stream of the nation's culture?

Explanations may vary, but in reality the phenomenal appeal of westerns—and the brainwashing accomplished by their myths—was widened with the advent of television. For much of the 1950s, eight out of ten prime-time television shows were serialized westerns based on variations of the Wyatt Earp "epic," and Hollywood's studios were grinding out a new cowboy movie almost every week. This mythmaking caper was put in perspective by William Kittredge, head of the University of Montana's creative writing program, when he described it as "art designed for the widest possible audience, all of America and the world overseas, and as such it isn't about anybody really, and it's not centered anywhere actual."

After a half-century of screenings, the clichés depicted in westerns had acquired such authenticity that theaters became defacto classrooms where celluloid legends were transformed into historical facts. Only a few western historians challenged Holly wood's mythmakers, and they found themselves spitting into stiff breezes whipped up by Hollywood's wind machines. Here is Larry McMurtry's description of the barrier these debunkers faced: "The romance of the West is so powerful you can't really swim against the current. Whatever truth about the West is printed, the legend is always more potent."

When Robert Dykstra presented the findings of his meticulous study of violence in the West to a Sun Valley symposium titled "Western Movies: Myths and Images," Henry King, director of a "classic" western, *The Gunfighter,* delighted the audience by rebuking "the professor" and denigrating his facts. Efforts by historians to put western violence in perspective encountered opposition not only from moviemakers but also from members of their own profession who glorified gunfighters as seminal figures of western history.

2 Living in the West

How might we best live in this land? How should we make ourselves at home here, rather than seeing ourselves as just passing through a space we aim to exploit and then leave? How might we adjust our lives to fit the land's patterns rather than destroy them? And with what non-human creatures do we share our home? The essays in this section explore such difficult questions through stories whose topics include creating a dirt floor, fighting pollution, admiring bison, and thinking about what might be lost and what retained if a beloved place were to be taken by wildfire.

Reflections in Mud

Stanley Crawford
from *The River in Winter:*
New and Selected Essays

In this witty essay, Stanley Crawford reveals how the constant
upkeep demanded by his home's adobe floor parallels the mindful
living he has undertaken on a small farm in northern New Mexico
for more than thirty years.

The thing about an adobe floor is that it would be cheap. Cheap as in free.

Rose Mary and I had gone through the last of the one-time-only movie money from my first novel, converting it into two acres of land, construction supplies, and an old flat-bed Chevy to haul everything around. Financial swords into ploughshares. One-time-only because they never made the movie.

These were the good old days of free-for-the-asking dirt roofs, adobe bricks, mud plaster, and mud floors. All you had to own was the dirt, and not even all of that, because foraging for sand, rocks, clay was still permitted on BLM land, which our two acres adjoined at the bottom of the drive to the south, where the sand was, and above the acequia to the north, where the rocks and clay were.

So, the mud floor. The basic mix was the dirt from the future front yard, which had served well for our adobe bricks and for the dirt roof, and somewhat less well for the mud plaster, for our first two rooms, which we built June through October with the help of friends. I mixed the mud for the floor in a big old con tractor's wheelbarrow, steered the heavy loads inside through the living room doorway, tipped up the handles and poured; and then Rose Mary spread, troweled, and smoothed the thick gooey mass over a base of white pumice (for insulation, free from the Pajarito Plateau near Los Alamos), on her hands and knees. Our small children, one and three, bundled up against the cold, pressed their noses against the milky plastic of the temporary windows or watched from the kitchen doorway. We worked from early morning until after dark, which we were able to do, still being young in early December 1971.

We made three mistakes. We poured the floor too thickly, we poured the thick floor too late in the season, and we got the mix wrong for the too-late, too-thick floor. It took forever to dry. In December we moved in on a carpeting of tar paper over the firm but still damp mud. When it finally did dry out, our winter housesitters, who had helped us make our adobe bricks, swept the floor so vigorously that the quarter-inch cracks became a network of fascinating little arroyos, which we bridged with thick hand-me-down throw rugs. Oh, pioneers.

In spring, we patched the worst areas with a sandier, less crack-prone mix, kneading it back into one piece, then sealed it with a liquid with the promising name of "floor hardener." The traditional binder was ox blood but there appeared to be no ready source of oxen anymore—and then there was the more delicate question of how, as then vegetarians, we could justify the slaughter. The effect of all this—wavy walls, lumpy floors, rough-cut ceiling, rough-trimmed vigas—was to inspire some old friends on their first visit to our new house to ask, "How did you find this hundred-year-old adobe?"

Since then we have smoothed out much of the original roughness: professionally applied hard plaster on the walls in some of the rooms, some of the floors torn up and re-laid, and all the leaky, cold dirt roofs replaced with fiberglass insulation and metal roofing.

But the living room adobe floor remains a flawed, ancient presence. I say ancient not because it is all of thirty years old but because a kind of peculiar reversal has taken place. During construction, the house was surrounded by earth worn barren and compacted by footprints and tire tracks. Now, out the windows, you see only the acequia-fed lushness of orchard, flower bed, and lawn. The primordial barrenness of stone and dry earth is now inside, a rectangular slab the color of leather or chocolate, with the textural irregularities of stone, or skin, or parchment, or lichen, or crusts of bread, or of wood worn and resurfaced and patched and roughly burnished, or of cuneiform tablets. In late afternoon when the low slanting light picks out the irregularities, the mud floor becomes a monolithic presence suggesting that the room was built around it.

I have seen carefully and wisely laid adobe floors, which look little more interesting than concrete, lacking the geological quality of a history of corrected ineptitude. Our floor is a record of its accidents. You can make out where the original cracks once were, where they have been filled, and where potholes dug by the iron feet of our first cheap furniture have been patched with a slightly different mix, where new hairline cracks are opening up, places where the floor has been pitted and refilled.

We have repaired it a half dozen times, sometimes with clay brought back from road cuts above Abiquiu or most recently eastern New Mexico, although these deep reds all but disappear under the darkening effect of the linseed oil we occasionally seal the floor with. Last summer we completely emptied the living room and I patched all holes and cracks, using fingers to push the wet mud into cracks and a sponge for smoothing, then sanding it all down with a dry rag the next day. After a careful sweeping, Rose Mary brushed in linseed oil on hands and knees, sealing and darkening the powdery taupe-khaki surface, which we were able to re-inhabit in about a week.

There are times when I have fretted over the unevenness of the floor, but in repairing it again last summer I realized that under our wear and tear it will continue to evolve in ways that other surfaces within the house will not, surfaces that will be recovered, smoothed down, painted over, again and again. The history inscribed in the surface of our mud floor is a version of the history of the house we built with our own hands and of our lives in it since 1971. I re-read it often in tiny, granular episodes, during moments of rest, staring into space, daydreaming, and in those pauses between the major domestic events of the day. The white spot left by one of the three fledgling magpies we have raised. Pock marks and hairline cracks made by the heat in front of the fireplace. A rough arc, where we commonly move back and forth an old cottonwood log that serves as a footstool.

The floor is the closest I will ever get to owning a Dubuffet, my favorite painter, fellow student of the patina of surfaces underfoot. It reminds me of the days of baths in a tin tub on the kitchen floor of two -by-six wood mill ends, of years without running water, of all four of us and the dog sleeping in one room: it reminds me that this was the best we could afford. It has required a cash outlay of perhaps a dollar or two a year for linseed oil. And in its way, in the way of wear and patching and repatching, in its slowly evolving patina, the mud floor will continue to record the history of our steps and pacings, of things dropped and spilled and dragged.

A mud floor is perfectly sustainable, being infinitely repairable and finally recyclable. Some future owners of the house, our children or grandchildren, craving smoothness and regularity, may take a pickax to the earthen slab, and cart the four-inch-thick chunks outside— where I hope they will spread them out in the weather, letting the rain and snow soften them back into lumps of earth, exposing to light and moisture the tiny seeds hidden within, underfoot, all these years, seeds from which plants will grow again.

Bison Athletics

Dale Lott
from *American Bison:*
A Natural History

Naturalist Dale Lott gives us all things bison. "Bison Athletics"
focuses on the prodigious physical feats of these Plains icons and
the physiology behind them.

Even though they're imaginary, we can't imagine Elsie the contented cow or Ferdinand the flower-loving bull winning a footrace with Silver, the Lone Ranger's horse—and they couldn't. But Harvey Wallbanger, a flesh -and-blood buffalo, regularly showed his heels to racehorses in the440- yard dash. To be sure, these humiliated horses were not the fastest ever to go to the starting gate—in fact, many were among the slowest in America's racing stables. Still, they were racehorses, while Harvey was basically an off-therack buffalo: the one who happened to be handy when a shrewd cowboy decided to go into the buffalo-racing business.

Harvey's triumph would not have surprised the Sioux, Crow, Black feet, Comanches, and Cheyennes who hunted buffalo from horseback for nearly two centuries. While most of their horses could overtake one buffalo, only a few could overtake several buffalo in one chase. A buffalo's skinny rump and long front legs give it a long-enduring stride—a good match for a coursing predator like the wolf. It is an animal faster than, well, some speeding racehorses, and able to leap tall road cuts at a single bound.

Grazing buffalo show no signs of Harvey Wallbanger's athleticism. They plod in short steps from one mouthful of grass to the next. When they move to water it's at a faster but still patient and economical walk. They lie down and get up with deep sighs and a cautious folding and unfolding of their legs that suggests the outcome is in doubt. Yet they are capable, at any second, of a memorable athletic moment.

I'm watching a mature bull standing alone on a dirt road on the National Bison Range. He's the only buffalo around, and I have set up my movie camera, so I'm watching him through the viewfinder—finger on the shutter button—wishing, as a man with a movie camera will, that the subject would do something footage-worthy. He stands broadside to the road's line of travel, his front feet at the bottom of the cutbank where the road is in a trough cut through a low hill to ease the grade. His right horn slips into the cutbank and cuts a horizontal groove. He glances up to the top of the cutbank, six feet above the road, cuts another groove with his left horn, glances up again, then—without seeming to gather himself—leaps to the top of the cutbank, lands upright on all four feet, and calmly surveys his new view. My finger is still on the shutter button, and I still haven't pressed it. I've just seen 2,000pounds of buffalo do a standing high jump of six feet. My breath is quick and a little shaky, but the bull is perfectly calm. After standing for a minute he plods off. No high fives, or twos for that matter, but his patient, confident amble seemed an understated celebration of its own—"Not bad for a big bull with a skinny butt, eh?"

At a cattle guard, the road through a fence is open to vehicles but not to livestock. You make a cattle guard by cutting a hole in the fence as wide as the road, digging a shallow pit the width of the road and (usually) eight feet long. Then you cover the pit with parallel steel bars three or four inches wide, an inch or so thick, and as long as the road is wide. Set them on edge about six inches apart, perpendicular to the alignment of the road. Wheels easily roll across it, but cattle, faced with the choice of a long broad jump or a walk on a surface their feet might slip through, choose neither and so stay on one side of the fence.

Management installed some cattle guards on the National Bison Range. They were working fine for buffalo cows and calves, but not very well for bulls. Bulls were getting past them somehow, and one day I saw how. A bull walked calmly up the road to a cattle guard, stood placidly on one side of it, then hopped—no other word would really describe it—across, landing on all four feet on the other side. This hop had to be long enough to deposit his hind feet on the far side of the cattle guard, so he cleared the width of the cattle guard plus the distance from his front feet to his rear feet, say another six feet, for a total of fourteen feet. A very impressive standing broad jump. Well, at least I was impressed. If the bull was impressed, it didn't show. He stood where he had landed for a quiet moment, then, with an air of "been here, done this," cropped a mouthful of grass from the side of the road and walked on—patiently and efficiently.

National Bison Range personnel countered the buffalo hop strategy by placing two cattle guards end to end. Now a bull would have to hop six teen plus six feet; and so far as I know, none ever did. But buffalo bulldom had not exhausted the arrows in its quiver. One day in breeding season I pulled my ancient Jeep to the side of the road, just after passing through one of these amplified cattle guards, and sat looking at the herd ahead of me. From behind came a distinct pinging, as though someone were tap ping something metal with a piece of wood. A bull's image filled most of my rearview mirror. He was in the middle of the cattle guard, placing his feet delicately, cautiously, one at a time but still confidently, so they were centered on the narrow bars of the cattle guard as he walked across with all the poise, and a good bit of the daring, of a man on a tightrope. I would not have been any more astonished if he had also been singing "Tiptoe through the Tulips" in a friendly falsetto. When he reached solid ground he walked past me and joined the herd, leaving me to ponder the demonstration of footwork finesse I had just witnessed and somehow make it fit with the demonstrations of brute power I had also seen.

For while buffalo leaps and sprints are spectacular, walking is the athletic talent that brings the animals to food and water day after day. Bison are roamers. Even in the confined spaces where they live today, they will travel ten or twelve miles overnight. On the Great Plains they may have traveled hundreds of miles from season to season—perhaps searching for a better place to spend the winter, or for a location with fewer human beings. They surely gained something from each step of those journeys, but (and here is where a physical feat is required) to be profitable each had to gain them enough to offset its costs. And the cost is high; bulls weigh about a ton. When a vehicle that size is fueled with blades of grass, every blade has to count. So the athletic challenge becomes like one of those competitions to see how far a vehicle can travel on a gallon of gas. It's all about efficiency—getting the most out of every drop of gas or blade of grass.

Why is it that an animal that runs so fast walks so slow? It's all about energy. Buffalo, and just about everything else that walks, set a pace that matches the natural period of the pendulum constituted by its leg. A buffalo's leg, like yours and mine, swings forward and back as the animal walks, so it's a pendulum. The key point is that every pendulum has a most efficient swinging speed, the speed at which it uses the least energy to complete a cycle: that's its natural period. When you walk at your leg's natural period, a good bit of the energy that moves a foot forward at each step comes from your leg's pendulum swing; in this way, each time a foot swings forward it's recovering part of the energy invested in the previous step. At its natural period pace a buffalo, or any other four-footed beast, can recover 35 to 50 percent of the energy put into each stride. But when it comes to walking, two legs are better. Bipedal striders (creatures like ostriches and us) recover more, maybe as much as 70 percent, of each stride's energy just by walking naturally.

How fast is that? A pendulum's natural period is determined by its length, but something a little tricky happens here. Suppose you found a bison whose hind legs happened to be the same length as yours and you walked beside it (at a safe distance), matching it stride for stride as it walked to water. Strange as it seems, you would not both be walking most efficiently. Your legs and his are the same length as legs, but not as pendulums—the "length" of a pendulum is determined by the distribution of its weight. The closer a pendulum's weight is to the place where it pivots, the shorter the pendulum and the shorter its natural period. A buffalo's legs are heavier at the top and skinnier at the bottom than yours, so its natural period is faster. You'd have to hurry your pace to keep up. How much you'd hurry would depend partly on your choice of shoes that day. Featherweight footwear would make your leg a significantly shorter, faster pendulum than would a five-pound pair of waffle-soled, insulated mountain boots. Come to think of it, moccasins would be about the best choice you could make.

But you can bet your best moccasins that Harvey Wallbanger didn't walk away from those racehorses. Both parties were galloping flat out for a quarter of a mile, and both could gallop—a little more slowly, to be sure—for miles and miles, as most hoofed animals can. How do they get the energy? By conserving it. This illustrates not the pendulum effect, since the bison's legs are moving much faster than their natural period, but more a pogo stick effect. As their feet land, they store the force of gravity in tendons and ligaments threaded the long way around the joints in their legs. When their legs flex with gravity, those ligaments and tendons stretch like the spring on a screen door, and that energy is recovered as the leg straightens for the next step. Imagine a door spring attached at one end to the back of your knee, stretched down the back of your leg over your heel along the sole of your foot, and attached at its other end to the bottom of your toes. If you ran on your toes and flexed your ankle with every step the spring would store energy as you landed on your foot and return it as you strode ahead. That's one of several springs in a hoofed animal's leg and foot—sort of an elaborate pogo stick. (But it's also different from a pogo stick, which stores energy by compressing a coil spring; a tendon stores energy by stretching.) Sheep can recover about 30 percent of their running energy this way, and camels may recover 50 percent. Buffalo fall somewhere in that range.

We humans don't have the feet for this feat. Bison are always on their toes: that joint about a third of the way up their leg isn't a backward knee but the heel of their foot, and the tendon from their real knee to their toes is long and stretchy.

Bison athleticism isn't all track-and-field events and efficiency contests. They fight, too (at least the bulls do), and power alone won't win a fight or even get a contender out of one alive. A bull has to twist and turn —quickly enough to protect his own flanks, quickly enough to get a horn into his opponent's flank. Selection is intense. Bulls are wounded every breeding season, and in most years 5 or 6 percent of the mature bulls in any population die of their wounds.

So the bulls are built to be quick in battle. To protect their body with their head, they need to pivot around their front feet. They have a great form for that function: much of their weight is centered over their front legs—their diminutive rear end is balanced in part by their massive head and neck. And the weight of their head is partly suspended from a point above their shoulders. There, rays of bone a foot long (called vertebral processes) project up from their vertebrae and anchor a tendon that attaches to the rear of the skull. This efficiently supports the transfer of their head's weight to their front feet, on which they pirouette on the sod like a hockey player on ice.

When I started to study buffalo a colleague said, "But they're just humpbacked cows!" Both walk on four legs, eat grass, and ruminate, but cattle were selected in a competition to supply milk and meat to humans cheaply and safely. Bison were selected in a competition to produce more bison—a competition in which the better athlete wins. That competition honed their shape and substance from small haunches to high hump, from size and strength to agility, from speed to stamina.

People sometimes say the competition in which bulls won breeding rights selected the "best" bulls, suggesting they do everything well. In fact, their specialization has cost them. One day I watched three mature bulls and a young one chase a cow. For the first 200 yards the older bulls ran easily, their long hair flowing in the wind. They even tried to mount the cow at a full gallop. But when the cow and the young bull circled back, still at a full gallop after a long run, the mature bulls followed at a wobbly walk, tongues hanging out and sides heaving. They were just too big to keep up the pace the smaller animals set. Natural selection has compromised much else to focus the bulls on one goal—forcing other bulls aside at tending time. It is then—when the bull moves to his task, beard swaying and pantaloons bouncing, belly lifted in an arch as he bellows a challenge—that he is perfect. And he is magnificent.

Savage Basins

Ann Ronald
from *GhostWest:*
Reflections Past and Present

Ann Ronald explores a "West haunted by its own histories." In this excerpt, she visits an abandoned mining town above Telluride to imagine the challenging home life of the Tomboy Bride.

With one hand lightly resting on the steering wheel and the other holding a cellular phone, Dave Rote of Dave's Jeep Tours slouched nonchalantly in the driver's seat and maneuvered his dusty Silverado up the narrow grade. To the left, an almost perpendicular rock wall stiffened upward. To the right, a drop of perhaps two thou sand feet plunged toward emptiness. Sitting in the open-air back of the truck, dust blowing in my face, I couldn't decide where to look.

Forward, I could watch red-shirted Dave finish his phone conversation, toss his black cowboy hat onto the passenger seat, then gesture toward the distant horizon. Space dropped off into space. I couldn't be sure if the front tire was holding steady in the track, if the steering wheel was steady in his hand. Reminding myself that Dave would be out of business if he bounced customers into infinity, I nonetheless shuddered with the rock ruts in the road.

Backward, I could watch the track recede, the orange summer paintbrush climb the cliff, the dust swirl in circles, the tangible earth. Occasionally I made myself glance the other way, nod at the view, survey the distant peaks, acknowledge the increasing depth of Telluride below. Mostly, though, I just hung on, past Royer's Gulch, alongside Whispering Jim's deserted shack, past the old Smugglerpost office, alongside ruined foundations clinging to the cliff, and then under the profile of the Elephant.

Dave's Jeep Tours turns into Dave's Snowmobile Tours in the winter. One customer from southern California asked if he brought snowmobilers up here. "No way," Dave answered. "Too dangerous. Too many avalanches." The Silverado slid past the Elephant's buttress, the steepest avalanche chute on the Tomboy Road, now July green and cobbled black instead of January white. "Too dangerous," our driver repeated as he wedged us around a dark blue Ford Explorer coming down from the basin ahead. Explorer on the inside; Dave's Jeep Tours on the outside. I closed my eyes until I thought we were safe.

"Too dangerous." In 1906, however, more than twelve hundred people lived where we were headed on this dusty afternoon. Despite the avalanche danger, the mines in the Savage Basin operated non stop, through summer sun and winter snow. The miners calculated the risks, took a few precautions, and went on about the business of extracting valuable ore from the earth. They cabled the Smuggler boarding house and mine offices against the side of the cliff, keeping it tightly bound beside the Elephant's chute. They erected a series of tramways to swing ore and men more quickly and easily across the steepest slopes. They dug tunnels both in the rock and through the snow.

While most of the workers lived permanently at the numerous mine sites dotting the landscape, other men traveled the precipitous route regularly. Mules brought supplies up a Tomboy Road that was narrower then, rarely wide enough for one team to pass another, never wide enough for a Silverado to pass an Explorer. Those men would have scoffed at my fear. So would their wives.

A few intrepid women made their homes in the Savage Basin, which once boasted the highest YMCA in America. Families lived there, children attended school. There Harriet Fish Backus began her married life, living nearly 11,500 feet above sea level through four storm bound winter seasons and summer reprises between 1906 and 1910. She rarely traveled the Tomboy Road back down to Telluride. "Too dangerous," perhaps.

The narrative of Harriet's early years with her husband, George, starts like this chapter does, en route to the basin. Harriet's trip takes place in December, however, not July; she rides in a horse-drawn sled, not a modern four-wheel-drive vehicle. "Steeper and steeper we ascended," she writes, "and deeper plunged the gorge beside us. An occasional glimpse was all I dared take. Only a few inches separated the sled from the menacing drop below." Snow falls, softly at first and then quite heavily. Farther up the trail, the driver reports "a stroke of luck." Part of the Elephant just slid. "If we had got here a little sooner it would've been the end of us," he announces. Harriet, clutching George's hand, responds through chattering teeth. "How can we get through?"

On that first frightening expedition and on others described in Harriet's 1969 reminiscence, *Tomboy Bride,* they manage. Every winter trek is dangerous. One time, near the lower tunnel, her horse slips on the ice. "For one heart-rending instant Bird's hind foot pawed the air above the thousand-foot drop. Only his God-given instinct and sharp reaction saved us both," she shudders. Leaving the basin for the final time, she describes how the horses crept past the Big Elephant, how "we could feel its menace." To the end, she fears "the treacherous snow-covered trail."

Although I personally felt no menace from the Elephant, with its summer array of flowers and its shattered aspen trees, I never felt comfortable on the Tomboy Road. Because of the relentlessness of the drop-off and the ever deepening chasm just a tire-width to the right, I never relaxed. Insouciant Dave, on the other hand, casually traces the summer route to and fro every day, driving passengers from Telluride to Tomboy, the largest abandoned mine in the Savage Basin, one-time home of Harriet Fish Backus, and site of substantial gold and silver operations in the early years of the twentieth century.

Actually, the Tomboy ruins are a popular stopping place on a wellused jeep route from Telluride to Ouray, Colorado. Any summer day, dozens of vehicles navigate the steep terrain, climbing more than three thousand feet in five miles to the Tomboy, winding sixteen hundred feet in just another mile and a half up to Imogene Pass, then dropping down to a different ghost mine relic at Camp Bird, and finally arriving in Ouray. The jeep route covers seventeen miles across the San Juan Mountains. By passenger car, on circuitous pavement, it's forty- nine miles, and faster. Tourists and locals love the dangerous challenge, however, and generally make the trip without incident. I wonder what Harriet Fish Backus might think of a jeepster traffic jam?

Dave takes most of his customers up to the pass and then back down the road to Telluride, but he dropped me off on The Flats, a level area above the Tomboy mine and in between what used to be the Japan and the Argentine properties. This was the early-twentieth-century residential district. While most of the single men lived in bunkhouses, the families lived in shacks on The Flats. Little remains now. In fact, the tallest structure on The Flats today is a $15,000 solar-powered out house, constructed for the jeeping tourists. That's where Dave left me with my backpack, left me to see if I could imagine Harriet Fish Backus's life in the Savage Basin. I wonder what she might think of a solar- powered outhouse?

I decided to follow a single ghostly voice in Colorado, to walk in Harriet's footsteps, to see what she saw ninety years ago, to contemplate what she remembered and what has changed. What could I learn, not only from the way she conceived of her own past but also from the ways she imagined the pasts of those who preceded her? What might I perceive differently? So I began as she did, letting someone competent transport a somewhat fearful passenger up the Tomboy Road while at the same time looking eagerly to the adventures ahead.

Although Harriet arrived in December, her welcoming scene was far from dismal. She describes "the brilliantly lighted buildings of the mill," and characterizes the ongoing sound of the sixty stamps as "a dull, heavy, continuous 'thud.'" In contrast, no electricity serves the Savage Basin today. At night, it's totally dark, and almost totally silent. A major difference between then and now, I think, is the non-stop noise of a sixty stamp mill crushing thousands of tons of ore to isolate ounces of gold. Harriet's basin was never still. Mine was resonant, too, but in a different way. I heard the rush of creeks and a patter of rivulets, the crash of a rock slide off the southwest wall, the scared squeak of a pika, the rhythms of rain. I also heard the grinding of gears and an audible curse, commercial jets overhead, and the flap of the wind against the fly of my tent. Sounds of commerce, then and now.

Because a well-traveled jeep road cuts through the Savage Basin, few collectible artifacts remain. The bottles, the broken dishes, the tools, the cabling must have been irresistible, for the earth has been almost picked clean by scavengers who have swept whatever was available into their four-wheel-drive vehicles. They even downed the electrical poles, felling them with saws in order to snatch the transistors, leaving twenty-foot armless stumps scattered on the ground. Unlike many ghostly mining camps in the West, where purple glass still layers and dates the dumping grounds, the Tomboy seems cleansed of itself.

I backpacked away from the outhouse and put up my tent on a bench above The Flats. From there, my view extended across the basin in three directions. Telluride was barely visible, though I could spot the new ski runs extended above the town. The weather wasn't wonderful. Squalls blew around the surrounding peaks, while clouds formed and re-formed like the billowed residue of dry ice. Harriet notes "few electric storms, none close or severe. Thunderheads were quickly blown away but often we could see lightning in the valley below, and heat-lightning far far away." I observed the same phenomena—storms that didn't settle in the basin, faint echoes of thunder with bolts of lightning striking far below my vantage point, and a great deal of precipitation that would be snow, rather than rain, between September and May.

The next morning I hiked to Imogene Pass. Though the old horse trail was regraded into a jeep route in 1965, it still zigzags steeply above the basin. Harriet and George once ventured up the trail to see Ptarmigan Lake, which was the water supply for the Tomboy operation, and to visit Camp Bird on the other side. "Trips between the mine and the lake were few," Harriet summarizes, "and rarely did anyone take the trip for pleasure." Now a county road crew plows the winding track between Telluride and Ouray as soon as is feasible. Only seven days before I was there, workers had finished cutting through thirty-foot snowbanks so that jeepsters could reach the pass easily. When Harriet rode to Imogene Pass, she imagined those who rode before her. "I was tingling with excitement," she remembers, "thinking of the challenge these formidable barriers had been to pioneers first trying to cross them." I wanted to do the same thing, to imagine Harriet and George. I was excited, too, thinking of Harriet's own challenges, her body rigid, her heart pounding, her tentative "I'm afraid to go," which she spoke as she urged her horse forward.

I've read a lot of first-person narratives and reminiscences of the American West. I've especially read a lot of women's recollections. Few are expressed with the joie de vivre of *Tomboy Bride*. Though she often admits her fears, she as readily projects curiosity about her surroundings and enthusiasm for new experiences. Harriet Fish traveled alone from San Francisco to Denver to meet George Backus, her husband- to-be. As soon as they exchanged their wedding vows—a day late be cause bad weather delayed the train—they set out for the Savage Basin. Once there, this remarkable woman sank to her waist in snow, laughed at herself, pushed her Tomboy Road fears away and thanked the driver for "a wonderful ride," then opened the door to her new home, a "room ten feet square which was the living-room and bedroom combined."

She learns to order food, every package and pound freighted up from Telluride. She learns to cook at high elevation. She learns that meat must thaw before roasting, and experiences the hazards of spoiled meat. She reports that their best canned fruits and vegetables would be unacceptable now, but no fresh food was available. Housekeeping turns out to be relatively easy in a shack with little furniture, or relatively difficult in a household shared with busy pack rats. One day she discovers long-missing potatoes, cheese, and chocolate stowed care fully in a box of prized photos.

When the Backuses move to another dwelling, a bigger place with two rooms and a tiny bed niche in between, Harriet and George pad the walls with newspapers, paper the padding with blue drafting paper, carpet the floor with denim. "The view was superb," Harriet enthuses. Best of all, "the important outhouse was only fifty feet" away. In a severe storm, however, the setting is not so perfect. "On one such day of gathering fury our unprotected shack shook violently and creaked." She worries if they dare stay there overnight, though of course there's nowhere else to go. "What kept the cracker box standing I'll never know," she concludes, while her "chattering teeth kept time to the rattling of the old stovepipe fastened by wires to the rafters." By the next evening the storm has abated and Harriet's point of view has brightened. "After the fury of the night before we settled down to enjoy the silence and beauty of softly falling snow." So the pattern of her prose continues, with moments of fear or discomfort immediately followed by longer passages of contentment.

A shack similar to the Backus abode still stands awkwardly on The Flats. The main room measures approximately 10' x 15'. The kitchen, nearly as big, has a lean-to alongside. All the walls are aslant now, but I could tell that someone had taken care to paper them with something green, and had painted the window sills a complementary darker shade. Two stove holes in the ceilings of the two rooms poke through a bent tin roof; underfoot, a dirt floor. I thought about living here in winter, through long nights and constant blizzards and loneliness while my husband worked twelve hours a day, seven days a week. Even as I pondered the difficulties, however, I realized "the view was superb!"

Clearly Harriet prefers summer to winter. Her summer descriptions are softer, quieter, calmer, more pictorial. "The bowl of blue sky over the cirque, sun glitter sparkling on the snow crowning the rocky heights, the velvet-green in the canyon, and far below the mesas of the San Miguel reaching for the lost horizon." Even the worrisome avalanche chute takes on a gentler mantle. "The Big Elephant, attacked by the sun," she writes, "rapidly shed his heavy coat of snow and burst forth in myriads of long-stemmed purple columbines nodding grace fully."

Certainly the wildflowers were in full blossom when I was wandering around the Savage Basin. The hillside where the Backuses lived was a nursery of colors. I camped ankle-deep in white ballhead sandwort which, as the days passed, gave way to yellow buttercups. Not only columbines but Indian paintbrush shading from white to yellow and from orange to fuchsia covered the grassy slope. Higher, where the swampy remains of snow still moistened the ground, marsh marigolds grew almost solidly side by side. I startled a ptarmigan family into a red -green cluster of king's crown. Chicks darted in four directions while the mottled hen squawked a dire warning, then skittered through the tufted grass. Harriet remarks sadly that, in her day, the chipmunks were too tiny and the marmots starving. "Cruel scarcity of vegetation took its toll," she observes. Nearly a century later, unoccupied ruins and jeeping picnickers must be more agreeable neighbors, for this summer's marmots were almost obese, and I saw healthy chipmunks every where.

So the basin changes and yet remains the same. Where Harriet could never escape the thunder of the stamps, I could often imagine myself distanced from civilization. Even the fallen towers, the broken cribbing, the shattered glass, the isolated brickwork, the rusted cables and pipes, the mining detritus everywhere couldn't detract from the summer serenity I found. The ongoing stream of basin visitors was easily ignored because few ventured far from their vehicles. A typical car load would pause at the mill site, read the sign, take half a dozen pictures, glance around the basin at the other remains, then hurry up the grade, low gears grinding, to the next photo opportunity or vehicular challenge. Some might stand around a little longer; some might eat lunch. No one climbed to the gardens of flowers and snow ponds exquisitely benched above the basin.

Living Downstream

Gillian Klucas
from *Leadville: The Struggle to Revive an American Town*

*In this suspenseful opening chapter, environmental menace
seeps across a high mountain valley in Colorado. Its source
is a legendary mine district, just upstream from a valley
of striking natural beauty and a scattering of simple and
hard-won homesteads such as Doc Smith's ranch.*

Doc Smith didn't get the message until late afternoon, after he had finished his chores and made his way across the snowy pasture toward home, his heifers watching his progress from behind a gnarled wood fence. It had been a good day for working outside; only thirty-five degrees but sunny, and the air at two miles above sea level warmed to a degree that surprised visiting flatlanders. Doc crossed the wide dirt driveway and climbed the wooden steps to his house one at a time, leading with his right leg, his left leg following stiffly behind. At the top, he stomped the snow from his boots and entered the cluttered hominess of the combined dining room and kitchen, the center of activity at the Smith Ranch.

The message Doc found waiting for him was from Dr. Dennis Linemeyer, the young man who had replaced him at the veterinary clinic. Doc was only fifty-two years old, but times were tough and the town could no longer support two vets. Besides, Doc had a ranch to tend. He picked up the phone and sat down at the dining table beside the antique woodstove that warmed the room.

Dr. Linemeyer told Doc he had received a call earlier in the day. The man wouldn't leave his name, but he had a warning: "Tell Doc Smith his river is going to run red." That was all the anonymous caller would say, but it was enough. Doc knew what that meant because something similar had been happening to the river for years,

27

though usually on a Friday night before a long holiday weekend and this was Wednesday. Doc had never been alerted before, and he wondered what that could mean. He went back outside and trudged three hundred yards down the driveway to have a look.

The Arkansas River, one of the longest in the United States, begins modestly on the side of a craggy mountain high up in Colorado's Rocky Mountains just ten miles north of Doc's ranch. It quickly makes its way to the valley floor and snakes southward, losing altitude but gaining momentum as it travels 120 miles through the wide Arkansas River Valley before turning southeast across the Kansas Plains to Arkansas and entering the Mississippi River. When Doc stepped onto his old railroad tie bridge that afternoon and peered over the side, he could see the river's rocky bottom through the clean, icy-cold water.

Doc straightened up and looked east toward town and the hills rising behind it and wondered what was coming. Then he turned west and headed back home—a compound consisting of his log-and-wood-panel house; a vacant 1870s farmhouse; several large barns, deep brown from a century of harsh winters; and a number of sagging old structures long since abandoned. Colorado's two highest peaks, Mount Massive and Mount Elbert, towered over his rustic homestead and the snowy surroundings.

Throughout the evening, Doc worried about the anonymous warning and continued to check the river, but found nothing unusual. After the ten o'clock news, he grabbed a flashlight and his coat and tramped through the snow to the river's edge for one last look before bed. Shining the light into the water, Doc couldn't see that the river was already changing, and in a strange way, he was disappointed. He had expected something to happen and began to think the caller had been wrong.

Doc went back to his house, climbed the stairs to the bedroom, and packed a few clothes for a meeting in Gunnison the next day before getting into bed. Lying in the darkened room next to his wife, he remembered all of the other times he had worried about the river and wondered what he would find in the morning.

Earlier that day, five miles east of Doc's ranch, rusty-hued sludge had poured out of an old tunnel cut into the hillside, a "Danger! Do Not Enter" sign affixed to one of the decaying wooden beams holding up the tunnel's entrance. The sludge entered California Gulch, one of many crevices dug into the mountains by glaciers that drain snow and rain into the valleys below. But this sunny winter afternoon, the gulch carried a vast toxic hemorrhage that cut a swath through fresh snow as it plunged down the hillside past dormant aspens and pine trees. It edged by the hard-knocks town of Leadville, picking up toxic strength as it flowed past the enormous mound of mining spoils that loomed at the end of Leadville's main street. The sludge continued flowing west, over silvery green sage; past Stringtown, a collection of trailer homes and run-down wooden structures; and through the shadows of undulating gritty black hills before entering Doc's beautiful valley. There it poured into the Arkansas River.

For days previously, the sludge had been backing up into the Irene mine shaft. The Yak Tunnel that normally drained groundwater from the Irene, among numerous other mines, must have been blocked by the rotting timbers and rock walls that periodically toppled over and prevented the contaminated water from draining into California Gulch. The manager of ASARCO Inc., the mining company responsible for the tunnel, decided it was time to go in and have a look around.

Nine ASARCO employees had ducked past the "Danger!" sign and entered the tunnel. With the light affixed to their hard hats leading the way, the men walked along the sludge-covered floor of the tunnel, their passage clearing a channel. Along the way, they encountered several areas of fallen timber and rock that dammed the flow of water and "slime," as the manager would later note in a handwritten report. In some areas, the stagnant water reached chest height. Working in the dim light with little fresh air, the men removed much of the timber and rock obstructions so that "a considerable flow was running" by the time they left the tunnel.

"None of the newer people enjoyed this trip very much," the manager wrote in his report. "We all got very wet, very orange and very cold. I, nor did anyone who made the trip before, quite expect the gravity of the problems we saw." The old timbers were in terrible shape, and the group agreed that more blockages within the year were inevitable.

It would be hours before the consequences of ASARCO's trip into the tunnel would be known, but they were devastating. The toxic torrent let loose consisted mainly of "yellow boy," a miners' term for the iron hydroxide that gave the river its rusty color, plus an assortment of other heavy metals, all dangerous in high quantities: zinc, copper, cadmium, manganese, lead, and arsenic. In recent years, the Yak had been draining 210 tons of these metals into the Arkansas River each year. California Gulch had long since been stained a permanent rusty orange.

Mining's toxic by-product came from the hills, but for over one hundred years it had been flushed downstream, unchecked and unregulated and out of sight to those working in the mines. And it had had a disastrous effect on the valley below. For three miles south of the confluence of California Gulch and the Arkansas River, through the Smith Ranch, the Arkansas River had long been considered a dead zone. No wildlife, most notably fish, could survive the metallic-tainted water. For another sixty miles beyond the dead zone, few trout survived more than a couple of years.

Ranchers had been using the Arkansas River to irrigate their land and water their livestock for generations. The accumulation of metals from 130 years of mining the hills had taken its toll; acres of barren ground pocked the meadows, and the grass that did grow there was so mineral-rich that the foals and calves that grazed on it were poisoned to death.

The Smith family had taken the brunt of the contamination, living in the midst of the dead zone since 1879, when Doc's grandfather, Henry, first homesteaded 160 acres of verdant meadows below two vast mountain peaks and the sparkling Arkansas River meandering right through the middle of it. Back then, timothy grass grew "as high as a horse's back," and Henry and his new neighbor, Huey Young, built an irrigation ditch, still known as the Smith-Young Ditch, to spread the clean, cold river water over the meadows. Doc's grandfather was in business, making hay for the area's milk cows and the mules that lived underground in the mines. But over the last twenty years of the eighteen hundreds, more and more waste from the mining operations was dumped into the Arkansas River, which soon became "rolling mud," as Henry described it. Timothy grass turned to stubble, and Henry's once-successful hay business floundered. Even then, Doc's grandfather knew the source of his problems. To prove it, he gathered up soil from his meadow and sent it over the mountains to the Agricultural College of Colorado in Fort Collins. The reply—the Environmental Protection

Agency (EPA) would excitedly refer to it as "The Letter" seventy-five years later—dated July 30, 1906—confirmed Henry Smith's fears.

Dear Sir:

The sample of soil and letter pertaining thereto were duly received. The letter has been misplaced so I cannot answer your questions except as I remember them. You apparently know exactly the cause of your trouble i.e. mine water and mill tailings. The sample sent is so rich in the latter that we would think that you must have gathered the sample from the bottom of a ditch or stream. There is a large amount of soluble iron and zinc salts present either of which are injurious in such quantities.

Yrs, W P. Headde

Mining, bringing fame and fortune to those just a few miles away, was killing Henry's meadows and his livelihood. All he could do was build another irrigation ditch, the Smith Ditch, to carry water from a creek farther west in the mountains. It was a long haul, but the water was cleaner, diluting the effects of the Arkansas River, and grass grew again, though not as it had thirty years earlier. Henry's son, Jim— Doc's father—decided livestock would be more profitable, and the ranch began raising cattle. But by 1940, as Leadville's mines increased production of lead and zinc in anticipation of World War II, the calves and foals began to come up lame and many died. And the cows were too skinny, unable to bulk up like cattle at the southern end of the valley. Jim Smith couldn't give his problems a name, but he knew they stemmed from the same place his father's had—mining waste draining out of the hills, and he would tell his son that many times over the years.

His son, Bernard—to become "Doc"—had grown up on the ranch watching the livestock suffer and he decided to become a veterinarian. He returned from school in the mid-1950s to be Lake County's only vet, starting his practice in the basement of a new house, built just a few yards from the 1870s farmhouse he and his father had grown up in. Doc was small in stature with a fine-boned handsomeness and well-groomed like his father and grandfather. In another era he would have been considered a "gentleman farmer," as his grandfather had once been. Doc had what his wife would later describe as the Irish Catholic belief that the longer and harder one suffers the more points earned with God, something her German Protestant background didn't share. Doc earned a lot of points his first year back on the ranch.

The winter of 1957 had been cold—more snow and ice than normal, and the ground was frozen into slick concrete. By spring, the ranch was behind schedule; nearly May and the yearlings had not yet been dehorned or vaccinated. One day, Doc and a ranch hand were rushing to round up some unruly calves. "I was the guy who was always in too big of a hurry," Doc would recall. He turned his horse quickly on the frozen ground and all four legs went airborne. As the horse crashed on its side, Doc heard his left leg snap like a willow stick. It didn't seem too bad at first. The hardened mountain men made a splint and eventually got Doc to the Leadville hospital, ten miles away, a few hours later. But Doc had fractured his lower leg in four places and crushed the blood vessels. Rushed to Denver—four hours over Loveland Pass in those days—the doctors amputated his leg just below the knee. Only in his mid-twenties at the time, Doc would never fully recover, fighting feelings of inadequacy and gritting through the pain of working the ranch on an amputated leg the rest of his life, though he rarely let on and most people in town never knew despite his stiff gait.

Over the years, Doc earned a reputation for his patience, teaching young ranch hands to "cut nuts," the western tradition that gives restaurants the prized Rocky Mountain oysters, and for his acrimonious sense of humor, softened by an impish smile and a sense of tease in his gravelly smoker's voice. He brought to the ranch a redhead named Carol he had met on a blind date in college. Her lovely smile belied an even wickeder sense of humor than Doc's. Though she'd grown up on the outskirts of Denver, still a cow town then, Carol loved the ranch, and Doc admired her toughness. Their good-natured humor helped them raise eleven children. Carol survived the neonatal onslaught by becoming a laid-back mother and housekeeper. If future surgeon George ended up wearing dirty, mismatched socks to school because he hadn't bothered to pick up his clothes, that was fine with Carol. And she rarely wore her glasses in the house so she wouldn't see the dust bunnies gaining mass in the corners.

But the contaminated ranch left them so poor the children were sometimes allowed just half an egg at breakfast. A high-altitude mead ow should produce about two tons of hay per acre. "The best I ever got, when my wife wasn't pregnant and was working her buns off out there, was up to 0.88 tons per acre. You can't make a gosh darn living."

Their troubles intensified in 1971 when ASARCO opened another lead, zinc, and silver mining operation up on the hill, sending yet more waste through the Yak Tunnel and into the Arkansas River. Doc complained about the contamination in public meetings, which didn't make him popular with the mining companies, especially ASARCO. "I'm not sure when I began to have intimate relations with the bosses at ASARCO, but we swore at each other. I didn't take them kindly, and they thought I was a pain in the ass." Doc may have been a pain in the ass, but that was about it. With no clear regulations in place to stop the mining companies from dumping waste, Doc had no leverage.

But by 1970a nationwide environmental movement was under way, with the first Earth Day held in April of that year. Companies in all industries were being pressured to clean up their acts. Pushed by the public, Congress began to address some of the more egregious environmental problems, creating the Environmental Protection Agency in 1970 and two years later passing the Clean Water Act, with its mandates to clean up contaminated rivers. Doc thought finally something would get done. His persistence led to a meeting on September 20, 1972, in Leadville's plain brick county courthouse. There, twenty-five men—mining company officials, local politicians, and state and federal representatives of the mining associations, health departments, forest services, the young EPA, and Doc—discussed, for the first time, the possibility of cleaning up California Gulch.

Orin Diedrich, a well-liked and practical county commissioner, complained that "those who have taken money out of the mines in the past have left us with a mess." ASARCO officials, however, claimed that its mining operations discharged little or no contamination, and state officials, at that time, agreed. Denying responsibility would characterize the mining companies' tactic over the coming decades -long battle once government officials finally resolved to address the hazardous waste that extracting the Earth's resources left behind. The county would do nothing to hinder mining operations, Commissioner Diedrich assured the group. Leadville's economy was thriving that year but, as it had for a century, it relied solely on one industry, mining, and no one, particularly the local politicians, wanted to contemplate its end in Leadville. They could envision the economic and social turmoil that would follow. At this initial meeting, Doc and the county commissioners were the only ones advocating cleaning up the gulch. An official with Colorado's health department suggested that "maybe the best solution is to leave it lie where it is right now. With the proper amount of funds, the water could be cleaned up, but it may not be worth it."

Not worth it? Doc realized that no one, not even the state's health department federally mandated to clean up contaminated water, was going to do anything. Doc spoke up. He wanted to see something concrete happening, he said, not watch the issue die of indecisiveness amidst the mumbled "looking into it" assurances coming from the agency minions.

After the meeting, Doc stood up and stepped stiffly into the aisle. Three scowling ASARCO employees, as big as NFL linebackers, were moving toward him. He thought they weren't going to stop. "They're going to run right over little Bernie." Doc was frightened, but he refused to budge. He put his hands on his hips and said, with as much nonchalant friendliness as he could muster, "Hi. Can I talk to you?" Doc explained to the men that he didn't want to shut down the mines, just clean up the gulch. They glared down at him and brushed past, leaving him standing in the aisle. It was an unnerving encounter, one that he would remember vividly thirty years later as the moment he first understood the danger of antagonizing such a powerful interest.

The morning after Doc received the anonymous tip about the river, he dressed in a suit and tie for his meeting in Gunnison, said goodbye to his wife and kids, and went out to his car. He drove slowly down the driveway and rounded the bend to the river.

Doc braked hard. Though the river had periodically been discolored in the past, the scale of what he saw now was unprecedented. Doc made a U-turn and hurried back to the house. He didn't want to be late for his meeting, but he wanted to make sure that this time the discharge didn't go ignored. He quickly wrote out a list of places for his wife to call: the local sanitation department, the

Colorado Department of Wildlife, and especially the Denver TV stations and newspapers.

He got back into his car and, as he bounced over the railroad tie bridge, he looked at the colorful river winding its way down the valley. He knew the toxic concoction was headed straight for the pump station that carries Arkansas River water out of the valley and over the mountains to supply the populous Colorado Front Range with drinking water.

Doc smiled. "We got 'em," he said aloud. "We finally got 'em."

Grassland Calculus

John A. Byers
from *Built for Speed:
A Year in the Life of Pronghorn*

*John Byers details a picture of the pronghorn and the grasslands
they inhabit. This excerpt combines scientific and impressionistic
observations to depict the complexity and the beauty around him.*

Late summer arrives with signs of the turning year. Young
meadowlark males burble in their full drunken glory, hawk
kettles imitate columns of smoke, grasshoppers reign, prairie
rattlesnakes begin the long crawl back to their dens, and the elk males
start to bugle. The evening sky may expand magically. Canada geese,
not yet aligned in the squadrons that will form later, straggle back
and forth and begin their first plaintive honking. Pronghorn females
begin to shop for a mate. At 5 a.m., Orion rears up in the southern
sky. Winter, waiting in the wings, brings an occasional dusting of
snow to the mountains. "I'm coming," he whispers.

On a clear still morning in early September, I noticed a thin column of black smoke rising vertically from the base of the Mission
Range. The column was so com pact and unwaveringly vertical that
I felt compelled to look at it with my binoculars. When I brought
the column into focus I saw birds, not smoke. I was looking at thou
sands of hawks that had found a column of rising air at the base of
the mountains. Each bird had its wings set to ascend in a banked,
spiral path that kept it within the thermal. I raised my binoculars to
follow the column up and was amazed that it just kept going—far
higher than I could detect with my eye. Finally, I reached the top of
the column, which flared out a bit several thou sand feet above the
tops of the mountains. The hawks, now tiny specks, were leaving the
dissipating thermal to glide south. From that elevation, they'd be able
to glide for dozens of miles before they needed to ascend again.

Columns of migrating hawks that ride these thermal elevators are called kettles. Broad-winged hawks are the most well known kettle-forming species, and in the eastern half of North America, kettles of broad-winged hawks are fairly common. But the Flathead Valley is much further west than any areas where broad-winged hawks are ever sighted, so I am not sure what species I saw.

Late summer also brings the ascendancy of grasshoppers, the dominant herbivores. Six species in three different families make up over 90 percent of all grasshoppers that may be found on the Bi son Range grasslands. These are the meadow, clear-winged, migratory, red-legged, Dawson, and two-striped grasshoppers. When they hatched in the spring, the grasshoppers were tiny miniature versions of adults. Throughout the summer they have been eating and grow-ing and molting from one adult-like stage to another. Now they've reached their final size and have become winged, sexually mature adults. Soon they will mate and the females before they die will lay eggs in the soil.

Densities of 25 grasshoppers per square meter are common, and at that density there are approximately 412 tons of grasshoppers chomping their way through vegetation on the Range, compared to only 258 tons of bison, 5 tons of pronghorn, 3 tons of bighorn sheep, 44 tons of elk, 17 tons of white-tailed and mule deer, and 8 tons of mountain goats. Thus the tonnage of grasshoppers is about 120 per-cent the tonnage of big herbivorous mammals. One might suspect that so many grasshoppers would decrease the quality of the range for the big mammals, but Gary Belovsky and Jennifer Slade, ecolo-gists who were already working on the Range when I arrived in 1981, recently showed that grasshoppers accelerate the cycling of nitrogen into the soil, and thereby actually cause an increase in plant growth.

In some years, when field mice are in a population boom (field mice here and in many other locales go through regular cycles of boom and crash), they may contribute another half ton to the herbi-vore biomass. There are also hundreds of other species of insects that are herbivorous to some extent, as well as dozens of other species of birds and mammals that eat vegetation. Thus a conservative estimate is that the Bison Range grassland supports 1,000 tons (2 million pounds) of herbivorous animal life at this time of year, as well as the annual reproductive output of all these animals.

That's a lot of energy to be produced by an assembly of plants that never grow higher than your knee. But the plants do it year after year and the grassland persists essentially unchanged, silently harvesting energy from the sun to turn air into sugar, and sugar into starch and cellulose. The herbivores eat these sources of carbohydrate and convert them back to sugar, then oxidize the sugar in the same way that plants do to release the stored solar power to do work within the body. There is a loss of energy at each chemical trans formation, however, which explains why the annual production of plant biomass is at least three times the standing mass of herbivores. The same losses explain why the 1,000 tons of herbivores support only about 2 tons of carnivores (cougars, coyotes, badgers, weasels, golden eagles, northern harriers, kestrels, merlins, prairie falcons, snakes, owls, and several dozen species of insect-eating birds). This energy and biomass pyramid, with a base represented by plants, a middle layer represented by herbivores, and a top layer represented by carnivores, is typical of almost all terrestrial ecosystems on the earth, and the numbers reflect the multiplicative costs of energy transfer as one moves up the pyramid.

The Bison Range ecosystem is stable because the numbers of herbivores are regulated. Grasshoppers are regulated by the amount of summer rain and the consequent summer plant growth, and by doz ens of species of animals that eat grasshoppers. Pronghorn, deer, bighorn sheep, mountain goats, and to some extent elk are regulated by predation (mostly by coyotes) on the young. The current 5 tons of pronghorn on the Range would become over 300 tons in less than a decade if there were no infant mortality. Bison on the Range have no predators (bison mothers are belligerent guards, and even if the mother was absent, a coyote would probably be incapable of subduing a bison calf), so the population is controlled by the U.S. Fish and Wildlife Service, which administers the Range. Every year at this time the Range crew, riding horses, begins to move bison into the staging area for the annual roundup. At the roundup, individual bison are herded through a series of chutes. Many individuals are weighed, the young of the year are branded with a single digit on the hip to show the year of birth, and a certain number of adults are sold. The sale is by an earlier, sealed-bid auction. If you have a winning bid, you back your trailer up to the chute, and the crew loads a live wild bison into it. You drive away, hoping that your trailer is secure.

When I walk through the grassland at this time of year, the grasshoppers rise in small clouds in front of me. Meadowlarks, mountain bluebirds, kestrels, shrikes, and coyotes for the time being have little trouble finding a meal. Clear-winged grasshoppers make a loud clacking sound with their wings when they fly, and that sound is just enough like a rattlesnake's rattle that it startles me every time. "Stop jumping," I tell myself day after day and year after year.

But my encounters with real rattlesnakes prevent any habituation. The species on the Range is the prairie rattlesnake, *Crotalus viridis,* which is mottled green and brown and well camouflaged in the grassland. Fortunately, prairie rattlesnakes are reasonably well mannered. They don't aggressively approach, as some other species of rattlesnakes do, and when I step close to them their usual response is to crawl away quietly. But they will coil and rattle and strike if they are sufficiently provoked. So, if I step close enough to cause a rattle, believe me, I jump. I've never been bitten in 20 years of walks through the grassland, but I have occasionally stepped directly over a rattler. When a snake rattles from between my feet, I'm startled enough to prevent habituation to grasshoppers for quite some time. In late summer, I need to look carefully before I sit down. The snakes have been out all summer, feeding on field mice. Each snake has kept to a fairly restricted area, waiting day after day for its infrared detectors to go off, telling it that a warmblooded mammal is nearby. But now summer feeding is over and the snakes need to return to their dens while the daytime air temperatures are still warm enough to allow a cold-blooded creature to move. Each snake may have several miles to travel, so at this time of the year a rattler may be encountered anywhere, not just near the ridges and outcrops where they spend the summer.

If you have been to Montana, you know that the term "big sky country" is more than a romantic metaphor—it is description. And the evenings of late summer bring on such skies in profusion. On an evening in late August, I returned from the Range at about 9:00 p.m. The sky was dark to the west, and there was a steady rumble of distant thunder. Little whirlwinds kicked up dust in the driveway. I walked into the house and found Karen sitting on the deck that faced the mountains. I sat beside her and we watched as the mountains glowed with golden light that streamed beneath the approaching thunderheads. As the sun sank below the horizon, the wind picked up and the sky above darkened to that blue of the wet sand on an evening beach after a wave recedes. Five thunderheads slid around and above us. The bottoms of the clouds looked like a cobblestone street—these were mammilary thunderheads, indicative of strong internal winds. Now the mountains darkened but the cobbled clouds picked up the golden light. Within each cloud and between clouds, bolts of silver lightning flashed against the cobalt sky. The golden light in the clouds faded to yellow, and the bottoms darkened. Now only the tops of the clouds were lit as the first stars began to appear. No rain fell.

Preface

Ann Zwinger
from *Beyond the Aspen Grove*

Beyond the Aspen Grove was originally published in 1970, at the leading edge of contemporary concerns about living well on the land. In this preface to the 2002 reissue, with the giant Hayman fire drawing ominously near, Ann Zwinger reflects on everything she has experienced, learned, and come to love at her cabin, Constant Friendship.

Writing a prefaceto this reprint of *Beyond the Aspen Grove* takes on a particular poignancy this morning. I feel as if I may be com posing an obituary, for as I write this, whiffs of acrid smoke from the monstrous Hayman Fire, thirty miles away where Constant Friendship lies, seep through the open door of my workroom here in Colorado Springs. The fire threatens the land that was the inspiration for my first book, published thirty-two years ago.

For the last month of this dangerous drought year I've contracted to get trees cut and trimmed around the cabin, a Herculean task. One exhausted evening, after dragging slash all afternoon, I gazed at one of the most magnificent sunsets I've ever seen, a J.M.W. Turner watercolor centered with a pure scarlet sun that painted the undersides of whipped-cream clouds a luscious straw berry pink. As I watched, pink segued into peach and rose and peony, blossoming up to heaven. At that moment, one could believe in heaven. The next morning the land was so preternaturally quiet, the lake without a quiver, reflecting the piercing spring yellow-green of the freshly-flushed aspen leaves. I embraced the peacefulness that soothed the mind and healed the heart. At that moment, one could believe in peace. These glimpses of earthly paradise fortified me for what was to come.

At the same time another part of my mind was mentally cataloguing the essential versus non-essential, my list of what really mattered, engendering hours of toting, boxing, stacking, loading and unloading, manageable only with the help of unbelievably kind and generous friends. In the midst of all that, as I cleaned the backs of multitudinous pictures in preparation for transporting them, I realized that there was a fabulous natural history essay to be written on the denizens that live on the backs of pictures. But there was only time for a quick brush to get rid of the myriad spider egg cases, the frass from the beetles who left massive amounts for such small bodies, and all the moths who breathed their last clutched on a picture wire.

When we built up here almost four decades ago, we did not know that it was a risky thing to do so, or that Smoky Bear rep resented a good-hearted but terribly erroneous concept, a prime illustration of the Doctrine of Unintended Results. I am comforted that we've used the years here well, and a cabin made it possible to have learned so much about nature and ourselves. In all our years, here, we have never been threatened by wildfire although I realize now it was just a matter of time. There have been forty years of happy times, preserved in almost that many years of journals. I am grateful beyond words for those records. They describe meetings of moment, shared times with family and friends, good meals and many Thanksgivings with the turkey cooked in the old woodstove. They note the muskrat plying the lake with a mouthful of sedges, each summer's new bunnies, the quirky denizens of the stream, a porcupine making unsuspecting dogs miserable, the skittering chipmunks, scars left by elk barking the aspen, leopard frogs that no longer sing and plop into the lake under our feet, skittish Steller's jays, the surprise of grosbeaks and warblers migrating through, a pair of mallards that return like clockwork each April, deer wandering through in their alert but absent-minded way, the loquacious Douglas squirrels and, one summer's day, a bear that sat and cooled off in the lake.

Just a couple days ago—last Sunday—we had a blissful picnic lunch on the deck with friends. Alternating sun and clouds laid different shadows on the land. Sequins of light exploded across the lake when the breeze ignited them, the aspen leaves sparkled in fresh summer green. The day ended with a sense of relief. The fire, we heard, was being controlled. And when we left, I did some thing I've never done in the forty years of meals I've cooked here—I forgot the luncheon casserole and left it cooling in the oven. I envision it burgeoning into an unspeakably moldy morass. My first thought when I remembered where I'd left it was how disgusting it was going to be when I opened the oven. Now I hope there will be an oven to open and any smells will be divine.

In an act of dramatic irony, the fire exploded the next after noon, just north of us, engendered by high temperatures, low humidity, and a shift in wind direction. This fire has been, from inception, despite heroic firefighting efforts, a raging entity with a destructive mind of its own, pretty much tracking where it wished, goaded by high winds. Fortunately, we had already removed the treasures of hearth and heart. The next evening Constant Friend ship was put under mandatory evacuation.

All day today, on our fiftieth wedding anniversary, I've listened to the slurry bombers drone over. I had hoped that our anniversary present would be word that the fire was no longer dangerous. Instead maps and reports are alternately chilling and cheering, but one fact is unassailable: the burn still expands. My heart despairs for those people who stand to lose their only homes and animals. And for all the mountain flora and fauna, Abert's squirrels and the impudent marauding raccoon, and all the company of aspen and black-eyed Susans and sedges and rushes who didn't or couldn't flee.

For me there is an odd consolation that if we have to lose this place as we knew it, it was because of the mother of all wild fires, a holocaust that simply refused to be mastered by even the most dedicated and skilled fire fighters in this disastrously dry year. As I write this preface, I acknowledge the unexpected gift of acceptance—after all, there is no alternative. I have the journals that document our lives here. I've written about this place, recorded our own simple discoveries, drawn the plants and animals that belong here, collected the insects and pressed the plants, have partaken of the spirit of this place. I don't know when we'll find out whether or not we have all survived—the assassin flies; the Parnassus butterflies nectaring on the stonecrop that has just come into flower; the graceful white anemones by the stream; the white-faced hornets that built a soccerball sized nest last year above the deck from which the in habitants frequently took exception in a direct and painful way to Herman's using the door; the mountain chickadees spraying bird seed right and left; the contentious broad-tailed hummingbirds. Those essential visual experiences, those memorable snapshots, will remain, caught between the little gray cells—the land's gift to those who have taken the time to learn its ways and to have loved it so well. And no matter what, the clouds will still sail across an incredibly deep blue Colorado sky, the stars will still flitter, the lake will still reflect them like scattered diamonds.

Beyond the Aspen Grove always was the record of a time that could never come again because all of its inhabitants irrevocably change, and some of them were unmannerly enough to grow up, among them Susan, Jane, and Sara who, in *Beyond the Aspen Grove*, were little girls splashing in the lake or creating plays on the granite knobs, or sitting in the Whale's Mouth or fashioning their own adventures and today, feel at home in the out-of-doors because of those experiences.

I recognized, in a suddenly poignant way, when I updated the nomenclature of the illustrations in *Beyond the Aspen Grove*, that change is an integral part of this place: no more do Grass-of-parnassus and the delicate moschatel grow here, but now the noxious bull thistle does as well as the happier discovery of coral root orchids. And no more do leopard frogs plop into the lake, or muskrats forage for sedges; no more does the cadre of night hawks sweep the evening sky, or the Cassin's finches come to feed. This book may well now be the record of a place that will never be again, that will exist only in our words and our composite memories, changed into something black and brooding we can never know or understand.

In spirit, *Beyond the Aspen Grove* is the recorded essence of a place that can never be torched or destroyed because any of us who have been there will remember it, each of us in our own way, because it shared with us the charm of an aspen grove near a small lake fed by tiny streams, wind that sounds like a distant freight train as it combs through the ponderosa boughs, the clicking dragon flies and the loquacious kingfisher, the white-breasted nuthatch mincing down a ponderosa trunk that has just been cut down, and all its sights and sounds, all its reminders of the profound and in tense pleasures and pains of being human and being alive.

Editor's note: The Hayman Fire advanced to within a mile of Con stant Friendship before it was contained, and finally controlled, due to the magnificent effort of dedicated firefighters.

3 ❧ Working on the Land

Some westerners do still ride horses, move cattle, pull minerals from the earth, cut down trees, and hunt. But as the pieces in this section make clear, the realities of working on the land are complicated: we also wonder at wolves, philosophize over crosscut saws and grasshopper behavior, expect good manners on wild and public lands, and both hide and fear toxic pollution. While most inhabitants of the Rocky Mountain region live in towns and cities, here we listen to men and women who earn their living by working outdoors with rocks, plants, animals, and other people.

Sawmill

George Sibley
from *Dragons in Paradise: On the Edge
between Civilization and Sanity*

*George Sibley explores the sometimes messy but often spirited
intersection between land and community. Here he writes about
the work of turning trees into boards—and his discovery of an
unexpected portal into another world.*

In the realm of interesting things that confuse me and confusing
things that interest me, the relationships between trees and
humans are high on my list.

In almost all of those relationships, we humans come off as de-
pendents—we need the trees a lot more than the trees need us. At the
most basic level there's the oxygen they pump out. They aren't the
only source of oxygen on earth, but they are certainly an important
one. This is actually a mutual dependency since they need the carbon
dioxide we generate—and we have become substantial generators of
carbon dioxide, probably more than trees at this post-Carboniferous
stage of their evolution need or can handle.

But in all our other interactions with trees, they are serving us,
usually in some way that demands a high level of sacrifice from
them. Our least demanding uses for trees are when we use them for
shade, windbreaks, and aesthetic decoration—we actually do a lot to
nurture and protect them in those instances, and even to help them
spread into places where they previously weren't found.

But our other principal uses for trees are for fuel and shelter,
and in those uses the trees get "changed" in the most Biblical sense.
Fuelwood is still the number-one use of trees around the world, and
a lot of land has been desertified over time just to keep humans warm
and fed. Civilizations have fallen apart from that most elemental
"energy crisis."

Our own Anglo-American civilization suffered that energy crisis a century or so before we began to move to America. My surname, in fact, kind of implicates my ancestors in that energy crisis. I've parsed it etymologically: "Sibb-leah" is what "Sibley" came from (the Old-English "leah" became "ley" in Middle English). Both root words are in the dictionary today: one's "sibb" is one's clan or kin group; "leah" is a meadow. So "clan of the meadow," or maybe just "people of the meadow."

But take "meadow" back into my ancestral prehistoric Anglo Saxon England and Europe, which was allegedly so densely forested that an energetic and focused squirrel could supposedly cross the island going tree to tree. In that environment "meadow" becomes "clearing in the forest." And take "leah" back into the less refined grunts and sibilations of the Indo-European proto-tongue that birthed languages from India to Iceland, and you got a sound which underlies the words for "light" in all those languages—thus, "the place where light comes into the forest."

When the American Sibleys went into the great forests of North America—and we've been here since 1629—that's the way we, in part, justified our devastations: "letting the light into the forest" was what the loggers said they were doing.

So that is pretty exactly what my name means: Sibley, the Sibb-Leah, the people who let the light into the forest. Eventually we left England for new forests in part because there was no more forest to let the light into; it was basically all meadow; and people were sneaking out at night to tear up hedgerows, dis mantle bridges, because wood was still the primary energy source for heat and cooking—that big chronic energy crisis.

Coal—and the opportunity to expand into America—bailed us out of that crisis. But it is sobering to reflect that, if we project 400 years ahead—the distance in time we've come since that beginning of the current "Fossil Fuel Interval"—we are at what many prognosticators think will be about the end of the "Fossil Fuel Interval": no more coal, oil and gas in economically recoverable quantities. We'd better hope that, by then, we've come up with some substantial way to tap renewable energy sources other than wood. Despite an avowed love for trees, I have not really departed far from that ancestral pattern of "letting light into the forest." For maybe ten of my 60-some years

I have depended on wood for heat—and we installed a woodstove in our current "modern" gas-heated house mostly because I don't feel that comfortable depending on a bunch of capitalists a state or two distant to deliver my energy. (Suppose they get a better offer elsewhere?)

And for maybe a third of those years I have made part or all of my living from construction and carpentering, and I am not so naive as to not know where boards come from. Like all carpenters today, I have shaken my head, and cussed a little, at the quality of boards that come from the lumberyard today, as though it were the boards' fault that the boards are not better. I saw a "clear" (knot-free) 20-foot white pine two-by-twelve, still as straight as when it was cut, in the old sawmill museum at Cook's Forest Preserve near where I grew up in western Pennsylvania, and I felt the mix of lust and longing any wood butcher would feel who has dealt with late-20th-century two-by-sixes. Nonetheless, I continue to go to the lumberyard in full expectation that trees will have been broken to handle whatever need or desire I am carrying out.

Boards of course don't really look like trees. Our so-called shelters, in fact, have come to the point where they pretty much disguise and deny any direct relationship with anything so natural as a tree; to look at the smooth flat surfaces, straight lines and squared corners, and the effort to create a constant mild climate within walls totally independent of the natural climate outside the walls, one would guess that we are trying to establish spaces somehow independent of nature's way of doing things.

It's said there is "no such thing as a straight line in nature"—or a perfectly flat or perfectly smooth surface. That's not strictly true; I have a rock on my desk whose edges are as straight as anything manmade, and I've seen sheet mica that does smooth and flat pretty well. It is probably the most dependable characteristic of nature that it always violates, sooner or later, somewhere or other, any absolute statement about what it is or isn't. But it is certainly accurate enough to say that nature in general does not share our human fascination with straight lines, squared corners and smooth surfaces.

And the disconnect between tree and board that results from the way we transform trees into boards enables someone like me to develop, on the one hand, a reputation as something of a tree-hugger with a great love for trees and forests (thirty or forty generations of cumulative guilt), but on the other hand, to make a fair part of my living as a carpenter, turning the broken bodies of trees into one-family houses big enough to have sheltered whole hunter-gatherer "sibbs." So the question arises: Can one love both trees and good boards?

I was actually lucky enough to get a chance to explore that question in some depth. In the course of my freelancing and oddjobbing career, I often had better breaks at oddjobbing than I was having at freelancing, and in one of those times when I needed something to put groceries on the table (not to mention a roof over the table), the husband of a friend happened to need a sawyer for a small sawmill he ran on his ranch.

Luce Pipher was the rancher's name, and he was a story or two himself, but that's a story for another time.

Cattle ranching was Luce's first love, but he had all kinds of things going on the side to subsidize the ranching operation, and the sawmill was one of those things—a little two- or three-person operation capable of cutting maybe a couple hundred-thousand board feet of rough-sawn, sun-dried lumber a year, on the edge of Black Mesa (north of the Black Canyon of the Gunnison), from where the mill's trees came.

I knew nothing about milling lumber, or the machinery involved, but Luce wasn't that impressed by my ignorance—and I reminded myself that I did have a Liberal Arts degree, after all, which is supposed to prepare you for anything the world can throw at you.

"You'll learn fast, one way or the other," he said the day I showed up to work. "Just go slow at first and try not to wreck anything." He gave me a twenty- minute walking tour of the machinery, showed me how to turn the various parts on and off, and ran a couple logs through the saw to give me the basic idea, then went back to his beloved cows and left me to some intensive on-the-job self-training. I took it slow the first couple weeks; I was so logically and rightly scared by the machinery that it was a month or so before I started to be reasonably comfortable with those singing blades a couple feet from where I timidly pulled and pushed the levers and buttons that moved the tree bodies around and into their transformations.

The centerpiece of the mill was of course the saw itself, a circular saw four feet in diameter. It ran off a big old antique electric motor that was, in turn, powered by a big old antique diesel generator.

A set of belts and electrically controlled hydraulic elements pulled logs mounted on a carriage into the saw. Getting the log onto the carriage was all done by muscle power, with canthooks to lever the log around. But the saw was the point of it all.

The first time I looked at the saw close up that first day, it was in repose, and did not, to tell the truth, look that impressive. It didn't look flat and hard, like the blade in my little skill saw; instead, it looked a little warpedy, dished— alarmingly floppy, in fact. I mentioned this to Pipher that first day.

"That's right," he said. He went over to it, grabbed it between a couple of its chisel teeth, and shook it; the saw flexed, bawong, ba-wong, like a big pizza pan. "It doesn't stand up," he said, "until it's revving at speed—720 rpm."

Doesn't "stand up"? My limited experience with steel had left me with the impression of something solid, hard and rigid, but I learned—and was to have the lesson driven home often in the weeks ahead—that a piece of steel four feet in diameter, spinning at 720 rpm, acts more like the pizza dough than the pizza pan. Under that much centrifugal force, its outer molecules tend to spread apart a little farther than its more central molecules. So in order for a saw to run flat and true at its operating speed, it has to be carefully hammered into a slightly cupped shape at rest.

He showed me: We fired up the diesel generator, then threw the head-rig switch; the generator lugged, then revved as the mill's vintage electric motor over came the inertia of the saw and got it to turning. For about 10 uneasy seconds, the saw picked up speed with a sound that can best be described as beating on the air. Then, it visibly and audibly "stood up"—straightened out in its motion, and the sound of beating against the air changed to a smooth hiss.

It gradually occurred to me in the following weeks and months that, when the saw stood up, it became something more than just a spinning sheet of metal; it became the force at a gate between worlds— the world of nature on one side of the saw, as represented by the logs on the deck: rough, barky elements from that naturally evolved world whose shapes and textures were all derived from eons of adhoc cooperation and competition for light and water, accommodation to other plants, adaptation to challenges, and probably instances of cosmic genetic inspiration.

But on the other side, beyond the saw, were the logs transformed into boards: all lines, planes and hard square edges, for assembly into the linear and planar shapes and smooth textures that hardly existed in the world before man came along.

In the two-plus years I sawed for Pipher, I never really lost my sense of amaze on making the first cut on a log: There was the log on the saw carriage, and there was the saw; I moved the log into the saw's space,

and . . . except for the sudden increase of noise, nothing changed; it seemed as if the log and the saw were occupying the same space without affecting each other, holographic images just passing through each other—until I completed the cut and the slab fell away from the log, exposing the pale smooth plane and the log forever changed.

It reminded me of the pictures in my high-school geometry text: line drawings of Euclid's plane, passing like a pane of glass through cones and cylinders to create the parabolas and hyperbolas of the conic sections. In the book, the pictures seemed quite abstract, devoid of reality. But there in the mill, there was the elongated conic cylinder in the rough, shaggy, lumpy and uneven form of the log—and then after the first cut, a smooth Euclidean parabola imposed on the log. The abstraction was the saw itself, the gate between realities: The saw was geometry incarnate, the powerful realization of abstractions found hardly anywhere in nature but in the minds of humans.

I quickly learned, however, both in the sawing process and then watching the lumber sun-dry in the yard, that the transformation from rough natural tree to smooth geometric board was hardly total or perfect: A lot of the tree passed through that gate to haunt the boards. Knots from branches that were important to the tree were very counter-productive in the smooth planes and lines of the board, sometimes even falling out when they dried. And the struggles of the tree to grow straight up on a sidehill, against the pressures of snow creep, rolling rocks and other natural forces, resulted in inner tensions that all worked their way out in warps as the boards dried.

I learned that I myself had a great deal to do with how much of a tree's old realities came through the saw to haunt the boards in that new reality. The sawyer's first responsibility lay in keeping that whirling convocation of molecules that was the saw as close to Euclid's abstract geometric plane as possible. Mostly this was a matter of learning how, and how often, to sharpen the saw's teeth. These were basically little chisels, forty or so of them, a little wider than the width of the blade, that chew at the wood with a sharp sna-a-acking sound when they are sharp.

But when the teeth grow dull, or get chipped by a pebble in the bark (or some righteous ecoteur's nail), or even when they are not sharpened straight, all sorts of increasingly ugly things begin to happen. The saw lugs down in the wood, the machinery begins to strain. And if one side of the teeth grows worse than the other side, the saw begins to bend toward the dull side, wandering off into a warpedy plane that changes the dimensions of the board—but, worse, causes the saw to rub against the wood on one side or the other, creating friction and heat.

The saw always had a thin jet of water playing on it to keep it cool, but twelve square feet of steel rubbing all the way along a sixteen-foot log can generate a powerful amount of heat, which causes the hot part of the saw to expand, which throws off that delicate molecular balance, and the saw begins to beat against the air again—and if you stupidly try to run it into the log again, it can turn into the most frightening piece of powerful chaos I have ever approached, with a handful of snow or a cup of water to put against it, to extract the heat and again return it to Euclid's smooth hissing plane.

So I learned quickly that, even though sharpening was a tedious job that produced no boards, the quality of both the lumber and the experience of cutting it depended absolutely on sharpening. Hit a rock at, say, eleven-thirty and try to saw on through to lunchtime before shutting down to sharpen, and it would be one long lousy hour. If you ever buy rough-sawn lumber that varies more than a quarter-inch in its dimensions from one end to the other, you are probably buying lumber cut during an hour like that—lumber that was quite literally born in an atmosphere of "bad vibes." Don't build it into your walls.

I began to learn too that how I started into a log had a lot to do with the quality of the lumber. No tree, being a natural thing, growing out of naturally uneven and hilly terrain, pushed by snow and bent by wind in the "Intemperate" Zone, grows perfectly straight; they all have a little "crown," or bow; that is going to translate into a little crown or bow in the boards that come through the gate between nature's world and ours. The internal tensions of trees can be amazing. Cutting 6 x 6 fenceposts from the buttlog of a gnarled old sidehill Douglas fir once, I had the internal tensions of the log squeeze down so powerfully on the saw that it would have stalled and burned out the motor, had I not hastily backed out of the cut.

The trick was to try to peel the boards off the log in a way that would result in the board warping mostly along only one of its dimensions (preferably its thickness) rather than warping along both its thickness and width dimensions, which meant that the most important moment there at the gate between the natural and cultural worlds was when I levered the log with my cant hook off the deck and onto the saw carriage. I had to make a quick judgement before clamping the log with the "dogs" and sending it into the saw. By learning how to read the log—and caring enough for the tree that had been, to want the boards to be worthy of its memory—I learned I could minimize the extent to which the tree's problems in the natural world become the carpenter's problems in the cultural world.

I'd gone to the sawmill to work because Pipher had said he wanted to shut it down in the winter, which meant writing time, but I approached the work with a culturally-induced sense that it was a little beneath me—a world less intelligent than the one I, a college educated up-and-coming writer (so I still thought of myself then), was really fitted for.

But as I began to really get into the work—the geometry of the work—I began to realize that it was the most intellectually demanding job I had ever had, and in a larger moral sense, perhaps the most responsible. Aside from the responsibility of keeping my own limbs out of the machinery, I had a responsibility to the carpenters who would be stuck with the boards, and I had a responsibility to the trees, to do as good a job as possible in making their broken bodies at least useful, and maybe beautiful in the way that a good house, or even a good out house, can be beautiful.

I left the mill after two-plus years, mostly because business got too good. I went there in part because it was promised as a part-time job, shutting down in the winter, which I wanted for writing. But because we had a great functional assemblage of junk, and because I was basically a tree-hugger at heart who cared a lot about doing the work right, we were turning out good lumber. We had one customer—a developer/builder from Gunnison, who started leaving a trailer at the yard, telling us to just call him when we had it full of 16-foot two-by-sixes, which he was using in his houses. With half-dried rough-sawn lumber, you just use bigger nails.

But the upshot of that was that Pipher decided he wanted to run the mill year round, and there went the writing season. So I left.

In addition, I had begun to see how mill accidents happen, in my own growing casualness toward the potentially deadly machinery I worked a few feet from—like the fact that it had become a mundane act to go up to the overheated air beating saw with a handful of snow or cup of water to soothe it down. Statistics indicate that most mill accidents happen not to newcomers but to people who have been too long in the mill. Industrial workers start to put themselves through those gates, as it were—fingers, feet, hands, and all the knotty warpedy slices that come off the soul when one hangs around anywhere too long after starting to feel like just another piece of the machinery.

I loved geometry in school. I liked rediscovering it at the mill; but I am worried that too much time in a Euclidean environment—all the rough evolved textures and shapes of accommodative nature sliced and shaved down to feature less planes and predictable angles—might eventually reduce me, much as I reduced the trees, to some human analogy of the uniform standard two-by-four.

But still—I'll still say today, two decades later—I've never had a job before or since that required such a balance of mental and physical work and energy, and that particular level of dual responsibility, as that job at the gate between the worlds, the natural world of the tree and the cultural world of the board.

Good for Nothing

Jeffrey Lockwood
from *Grasshopper Dreaming:
Reflections on Killing and Loving*

*In this essay, entomologist Jeffrey Lockwood asks what we might
learn* from *(rather than* about*) these familiar insects—and offers us
a gentle challenge to reconsider our assumptions about doing and
being, science and spirituality.*

Introducing myself at social gatherings as an entomologist is almost
sure to generate interesting conversations. Everybody has stories
to share and questions to ask about their encounters with insects.
I haven't kept count, but the most common question I hear at parties
goes something like, "I know we shouldn't kill them all, but really,
what are they good for?" Them refers to the particular insect that
is the topic of discussion. After a moment, most people often suggest their own answer: "I suppose birds eat them." But somehow this
doesn't seem satisfactory, and they want me to explain the purpose of
mosquitoes, miller moths, or grasshoppers.

I admire our increasing awareness that all beings are part of
an interconnected whole and that when a strand of the web is
broken, there are often system wide effects. All of that is true, but it
suggests, however implicitly, that the purpose of this web somehow
involves us humans. The problem is that nature doesn't exist for
us, ecosystems don't care about us, animals don't generally love us,
and the universe doesn't really need us. Nearly two thousand years
ago the Roman emperor and Stoic Marcus Aurelius counseled that
it was important to "desire every one of your actions to be right in
your own judgment, and remember two things: Your actions are
significant, but the circumstances in which they take place have no
significance." This paradox is compelling: Each life is of infinite
value to itself and of no importance to the universe. To ask what

a life, human or insect, is "good for" presumes that value lies in utility, that worth is not intrinsic.

I know grasshoppers. I've dedicated my professional life to their study. Over the past fifteen years, I have employed many methods for learning about grasshoppers. Only recently have I begun to consider what I might learn from them. Science provides innumerable tools for learning about life, but ultimately one must turn to other ways of knowing to discover how we might learn from it. Fortunately, one can interpret a single experience from multiple perspectives; "good science" need not preclude intuitive insight or transcendent under-standing. An observation can provide information, foster knowledge, or evoke wisdom, depending on what the observer brings to the en-counter. So it is that the grasshoppers have taught me, among other things, the nature and value of nothing.

When I was hired in 1986 as an assistant professor at the Univer-sity of Wyoming, specializing in grasshopper biology and manage-ment, I was a competent entomologist. My only firsthand encounters with these insects, however, were as a child in New Mexico. My par-ents built a house on the outskirts of Albuquerque, and their land-scaping provided the only green food the grasshoppers saw in the summer. This afforded bountiful opportunities for catching grass-hoppers, which I housed in various containers or fed to the black widow spiders that lined the wall of the backyard, but these were hardly the experiences on which to build a scientific career.

So I began my university research by spending my first summer study-ing grasshoppers on the short-grass prairie just north of Fort Collins, Colorado. The site was ideal because it supported an abundance of grasshoppers (ten to fifteen per square yard), provided a wide diversity of species (thirty different kinds of grasshoppers), and was convenient (only an hour from the campus at Laramie where, at an elevation of 7,200 feet, summers are too short to generate many grasshoppers on the surrounding grasslands). I would simply park at a camp ground along Highway 287, climb over the barbed-wire fence, cross the weedy pasture to the north, clamber up a rocky slope, weave between the mountain mahogany shrubs, and emerge in a grassy field that covered a few hundred acres and contained a few million grasshoppers.

The ancient fellow who owned the land lived in a dilapidated set of buildings you could get to only via a bridge surmounted by two wooden tracks about eighteen inches wide. The challenge was to line up your truck perfectly on the dirt road leading to the ravine and then, unflinching, cross the bridge in a straight line. I suspect the old man didn't make the crossing often. In fact, except for the times I renewed his permission to access the land, I never saw him. I'm pretty sure I had his permission, but given his lack of hearing and teeth, I was never sure that he knew what I meant or that I knew what he said.

I spent hundreds of hours from June to September sitting on the prairie with a video camera recording grasshopper behavior. I decided to focus on just one species that year. The first rule of science is to simplify the problem, to isolate that which you seek to understand. I chose *Aulocara elliotti,* the bigheaded grasshopper. Although this is a serious pest of the rangeland, my interest was rather more pedestrian. *A. elliotti* was abundant and the size of a pencil stub, so it could be identified from a discrete distance. It has, as one might infer, an abnormally large head, along with a white X on its back and blue hind tibiae, or limbs.

Previous field studies on insect behavior had taught me that the greatest virtue of my summer's work would be patience. Remaining motionless to capture the behavior of the grasshoppers in an undisturbed state became increasingly difficult as summer progressed. The chill of dew-dampened mornings gave way ever more quickly to the searing heat of midday. The grasses set seeds, which took the form of variously modified darts that worked their way into socks, creases, and bootlaces. The sweat bees showed no gratitude for their feast, delivering burning stings whenever trapped between clothing and flesh. The muscular tension of holding the camera on my shoulder was creating a permanent crick in my neck. I took breaks periodically, but real relaxation came only when I became fully engaged in my filming, when I lost all sense of time and discomfort by total absorption in the life of grasshoppers. I didn't analyze the ten-foot shelf of videotapes until later that fall, but even in the summer I knew full well what grasshoppers did most of the time: nothing. Absolutely nothing.

The results of the summer of 1986 became my first published paper on grasshoppers. To be honest, only by a careful selection of particularly intriguing behaviors was I able to find enough activity in the videotapes to generate scientifically interesting conclusions. I deter mined, for example, that this species engages in territorial behavior, or at least aggressive intolerance of other individuals. Despite my focus on the times when the grasshoppers were "doing" something, for forty-three minutes out of every hour, they were not doing any thing. They just sat there on the ground or hung in the vegetation. I called this "resting," presuming they were saving energy for the real demands of life. Other biologists have ascribed such immobility to thermoregulation: If they are sitting in the sun, they are really engaged in warming themselves, while if they are hunkering in the shade, they are cooling themselves. There are some occasions when these interpretations are valid, as when they perch on top of grasses and turn perpendicular to the sun's rays in the early morning. But I suspect that most of the time when grasshoppers appear not to be doing anything, they aren't clandestinely engaged in pursuing other goals—they are simply doing nothing.

From the perspectives of ecology and evolution, spending hours engaged in doing nothing is difficult to explain. After all, these grasshoppers suffer a daily mortality rate of about 2 percent, meaning that only about one-third of those that hatch in the spring will survive to reproduce as adults. Imagine how your workplace would change if one out of every fifty employees died every day. If your doctor told you that you had a 2 percent chance of dying each day, that would mean you could count on even odds of being dead by the end of the month. Under these circumstances, an organism should be desperately engaged in securing resources and assuring its biological success—eating and mating—especially when the essential ingredients are presumably in short supply.

Ecology and evolution are implicitly grounded in the structure of human economics. These explanatory systems presume that the dynamics of life arise because essential resources are limited, thereby necessitating brutal competition. Economists seem fond of developing models that further assume that perfectly informed agents act with perfect rationality to acquire these inadequate resources.

That is, of course, a silly assumption in the case of humans, who are often misinformed and profoundly irrational. But insects ought to be well informed by their finely tuned senses, and in the presumed absence of selfwareness and individual volition, grasshoppers should be largely driven by the cold, calculating logic of natural selection.

Humans might invest according to their horoscopes, but insects ought to manifest behaviors that arise from simple cause-and-effect optimization of their fitness.

However, grasshoppers defy the economics that use either energy or genes as the currency of life. Grasshoppers are incredibly blase about reproducing or feeding. Sex appears to be an activity of modest interest, at best. Courtship and mating occupy a small proportion of their days; most of their encounters seem to be more antagonistic than romantic. In fact, reproductive behavior was so rare that I excluded it from my analysis and titled my paper "Nonsexual interactions in *Aulocara elliotti*." If we consider that grasshoppers often reach population densities of thirty, forty, and up to one hundred per square yard, surely they ought to be competing fiercely for their share of the food. But in my summer of behavioral recording, the grasshoppers spent only about three minutes out of every hour eating, despite the impending famine. There was no tragedy of the commons, no gluttonous devouring of a dwindling larder, no headlong race for each to extract the most food from the pantry. Indeed, in my many years of working with these insects in the field, I have encountered only three or four situations in which it seemed they had eaten themselves into an absolute shortage (a shortage of nutritious food may occur well before a field is literally stripped of all vegetation), and in these cases they simply walked or flew less than a day's journey to greener pastures.

What are the grasshoppers up to? If we humans were short of resources, we would surely battle for our share. We'd scurry about attempting to vanquish competitors, hoard supplies, mate feverishly, and, well, do much of what we seem to do in the modern world. But grasshoppers aren't humans. It is not even clear that they are operating under an economy of shortages, and if they are, there is scant evidence that they are behaving to ensure a competitive advantage. Why should they? If science aspires to objectivity, why is it appropriate to ascribe to other beings the values we use to explain or rationalize our actions? In a great subjective leap, we presume that competition for limited resources is the leitmotif of all living beings because this theme defines our own inter actions in and with the world.

The fact is that grasshoppers spend most of their time doing nothing (unless you count digesting, breathing, and being incidentally warmed or cooled). Our struggle to understand their languor arises from our approaching these creatures with the same question with which we approach one another: "What do you do?" It is as if we can define all worth in terms of what someone or something does. This assumes that value is instrumentally derived—things have worth in terms of what they do for us. Relationships are critically important to defining life, but they are not the sole measure of our lives.

If we were to reconstruct our scientific understanding in the context of intrinsic value (the notion that some thing can have worth in and of itself), a rather different interpretation of animal behavior, ecology, and evolution would emerge. If we seek to reveal the inherent worth and dignity of life—the intrinsic reality fundamental to Alfred North Whitehead's metaphysics, the inner being essential to Teilhard de Chardin's under standing of existence, the self that was the core of Ralph Waldo Emerson's meaning of life—then it is not surprising that a grasshopper might spend a couple of hours just sitting. I am reminded that Thich Nhat Hanh, the Buddhist priest, suggested that when people are hurrying about and shouting, "Don't just sit there, do some thing!" the crisis might be more effectively addressed if a quiet voice admonished us, "Don't do something, just sit there." Maybe grasshoppers would make good Buddhists. They certainly defy the Protestant work ethic (a failing immortalized in the children's tale "The Ant and the Grasshopper") and the cultural values that underlie scientific inquiry. Sometimes I wonder why we call our selves "human beings," when we spend very little time "being." Perhaps we ought to call ourselves "human doings" and reserve the notion of "beings" for the other creatures.

The do-nothing grasshoppers have taught me that science is very effective at assessing and understanding sub stance and activity. In terms of the interdependent web of all existence, science excels at analyzing and controlling the strands, but has little to say about the spaces. And a web is mostly empty space. There are ancient methods for exploring the space between the strands, but these methods are generally viewed as being not just different from but inimical to science. However, the emptiness is so essential to being that science must acknowledge its existence. Unable to manifest humility or reverence, we conquer the void by dint of language and faith. Naming is a powerful means of asserting control, and science has developed a rich assortment of terms to establish intellectual dominion over the elusive and unknowable. The mysteries that emerge between the strands are labeled as variation, noise, error, and chance.

This tactic would be more plausible if science had a test for randomness, but none exists. An appeal to randomness is a faithful prayer to the unseen. We can tell you what it isn't (randomness is the absence of identifiable pattern, the modern version of *terra incognita*), but we cannot assert what it is. Chaos theory demonstrates that sometimes randomness is constrained, shaped into a cloud of realized events by a so-called strange attractor. The origin and nature of these forces that sculpt order from formless chance are themselves a complete mystery. But what science cannot fathom, nature still man ages to exploit. At every scale, creative order arises from putative disorder. In evolution, random mutation plays a pivotal role; in quantum physics, probability waves lie at the heart of existence; in cosmology, nothingness gave rise to the universe.

A resting grasshopper is akin to randomness; it manifests a behavior that fails to fit any identifiable purpose or pattern that we expect to see. It is, as far as we can tell, doing nothing and persists in this state of meaning less existence for prolonged periods of time. To code the behavior of these insects, I designated "resting" as 0. When analyzing data, we differentiate between "missing data" and "true zero." Missing data are just that: empty, information-free spaces because we didn't look (or lost the data). A true zero means that we looked but didn't see anything. This system, however, presumes that when we don't see anything, there really is nothing there. Categorizing resting behavior as a true zero created the illusion that I knew there was nothing other than an immobile, impassive, nonfeeding, nonmating, noncompetitive, uncommunicative organism devoid of biological meaning. What it really meant was that I didn't know what the grasshopper was doing, or whatever it was doing, it didn't fit any of my expectations of what a grasshopper ought to be doing. The latter interpretation is certainly suggested by some subsequent work on feeding behavior.

Grasshopper feeding presented a bit of a problem. The amount of forage that the ecologists claimed these insects consumed could not be reconciled with the amount of time the behaviorists had documented as devoted to feeding. This wasn't a major biological controversy, but it was an intriguing riddle. The solution was incredibly simple, being a matter of changing expectations and assumptions about what other life forms ought to be doing. The dogmatic description of a typical grasshopper's day involved its basking in the early morning, feeding at mid to late morning, sheltering to avoid the midday heat, feeding in the late afternoon, and then resting throughout the night. Nobody had actually spent any real time trying to watch grasshoppers at night. After all, they were obviously active during day light, and staggering around the prairie at three in the morning seemed pointless, if not masochistic. But by capturing grasshoppers and examining their crop (stomach) contents over several twenty-four-hour periods, we discovered that on warm summer nights, these insects are happily munching away. In fact, some species decidedly prefer midnight snacking, which makes good sense given the risks of exposing themselves to predators while clambering around in the grass during the day. By partitioning their mealtimes throughout the day and night, a rich diversity of grasshoppers in a community effectively manages to feed continuously. Our discovery did not shake the foundations of science, but it did demonstrate how science can become a subjective projection of our lives, wants, and needs onto other organisms.

A good colleague recently told me that he had failed to replicate my findings of nocturnal feeding. He had taken several individuals of a single species of grasshopper from the field during the day, caged them in observation tanks, offered them prefabricated wafers of compressed grass throughout the night, and observed their feeding. They didn't eat the wafers, so he concluded that my "night feeding phenomenon" was an interesting but spurious result. I maintain that if you take an animal from its complex habitat, place it in a completely alien setting, and offer it a single, artificial food, then you probably can't say very much about what that animal and its community of related species are doing in the intact habitat. In fact, my experience with taking grasshoppers from the field and caging them generates a fairly consistent behavior within a very short period: They die.

First, dismissing unexpected results as spurious is a way to evade reality. In a spectacular metaphysical feat, that which science cannot explain ceases to exist. The life sciences are very good at induction and rather weak at deduction. We can predict the pattern or extract the generality, but we cannot explain the particular or ac count for the exception. For some matters this is fine, but the limit is obvious when we realize that each of our lives—and the lives of other beings—is ultimately a singular occurrence.

Second, science may be adept at developing and applying analytical methods, but you cannot see what you do not look for. Sometimes you don't even recognize you are looking through the wrong end of the telescope. Isolating elements of complex systems for scientific study is a defensible and useful tactic, but it requires that we ignore vast numbers of relationships. This approach generates valuable information and suggests plausible mechanisms, but it does not reveal ultimate explanations or assure wisdom. And so, in answering the polite and honest question "What is a grasshopper good for?" the ecologist in me wants to discuss the role of this creature in nutrient cycling, and the evolutionist in me wants to explain that it is good at replicating itself. But I have come to under stand that these are ends that we impose and values that emerge only by induction; the grasshopper is unaware of our goals and statistical extrapolations. We might as well as ask ourselves what our children are good for: Do we love them because they are efficient omnivores, effective competitors, successful phenotypes, genetic successors? These qualities give the right answers to the wrong question. The reason we value our children is not because of what they do, but because of who they are. That's why as a spiritual scientist, my answer is that a grasshopper isn't good for anything. Its presence is of no significance—an ultimate zero. Its value is in being a grasshopper, nothing more. The grasshopper just is. And that is enough.

Backcountry Ranger

Gary Ferguson
from *Hawks Rest: A Season in the
Remote Heart of Yellowstone*

*Most national park visitors explore no farther than a few hundred
feet down any trail. Not Gary Ferguson, who backpacks into
a little-known corner of Yellowstone and meditates on bears,
wilderness, hunters, poachers, and a backcountry ranger who once
saw Buffalo Bill's Wild West Show as a child in Austria.*

Cavan Fitzsimmons sits at the table at Hawks Rest—a smudged
felt hat cocked over his boyish face, a cheap fork in one hand
and a pocketknife in the other—waiting to eat a steak cooked
just past bloody off a plastic plate. A former football player, he has
the roguish good looks of a movie star with none of the effort. Sitting
next to him is his partner on this shift, Jason, a thin, wiry man even
more covered in soot than most, whose size belies his ability both
to eat like a bear as well as to spend hour after hour fast dancing
with a crosscut saw. "Had everything today but an encounter with
an endangered species," Cavan says, recounting a wreck two hours
earlier when a cross cut saw came off one of the mules, as well as the
usual trail work, policing dirty camps, catching people building fires
despite the fire ban. "Yeah, I knew there was a ban," one guy told
him at Two Ocean Pass. "But I didn't think there was much chance
of running into you."

Testosterone runs thick in the Thorofare, and one of the ways it
shows up in trail crews is through an obsession to do more work than
anyone else in a given day. Cavan isn't just a workaholic, some say, but
a work maniac. And while that may fit well with Jason, who can match
him step for step, other people Cavan has worked with this summer
have been muttering under their breath that he's one crazy bastard.
Several years ago, when it was just Cavan working the entire northern

end of the Teton Wilderness, he'd routinely ride 250 miles on every shift, trying hard to show as much presence as possible to outfitters. Three weeks from now his girlfriend, Sally, will come on board as a volunteer for an eight-day hitch—a chance, she figures, to see what her beau does for a living—and she too will nearly be run into the ground.

Perhaps in part because of their age, many of these seasonals still have in their pockets some fine shavings of idealism. The son of a horse trainer and a federal judge, Cavan truly believes he's making a difference here. "My mom was great," he tells me over a cocktail of vodka and Gatorade, trying to explain the origins of his can-do attitude. "When I was about 11 years old, I wanted a horse. But instead of just giving me one she gave me a broodmare, told me to find a stud horse and breed her, so that's what I did. She knew I'd have to care for that mare during her pregnancy, then raise the colt. Only after all that, once I had a relationship with it, would I be able to ride. By the end I understood something about the investment it takes to get what you want."

I offer to cook up the steaks and vegetables the boys brought in so they can kick back and relax, and once again the talk goes on until midnight. Idealism aside, Cavan does seem to struggle now and then—at least in the late hours, when the need for sleep is pulling on him—trying to reconcile what needs to be done on this forest with his limitations as a seasonal. The fresh order that just came down prohibiting hunting within 200 yards of a salted site—that one he knows to be more or less unenforceable, at least until the salts are clearly marked, and few people on the forest even know where they are. Besides, as LaVoy points out, if the law is meant to keep outfitters from hunting over existing salts, what's there to prevent them from simply creating new ones? No one even bothers to mention the most obvious problem, which is how less than a handful of people are going to patrol 300 square miles of land, showing up at the right moment to catch someone shooting in the wrong place.

If Cavan continues to make it in this free-for-all, it'll be in part because of his sense of humor. Over a dessert of cookies and M&M's, he recalls the time last year when he rode up on some one with his tent set up right next to a stream. Told that he'd have to move a hundred feet from the water, the guy unclipped his holster, turned his pistol around, leaned forward and growled: "Fuck you, pine pig."

Cavan says the pine pig part cracked him up, that he laughed so hard that in the end the guy ended up laughing about it too; before long the two of them were moving the tent. When he first started working here he was told by other rangers to "disbelieve pretty much everything you hear, unless you have clear proof it's true"—a piece of advice he now passes on to newcomers. With outfitters it's a game, he explains, always a game.

Last week he stumbled across a camp and found a huge fire burning, right in the middle of the fire ban. The outfitter tried to explain it away, saying one of his clients had fallen in the creek and they were just trying to warm him. "It was bullshit, of course," Cavan says, no particular rancor in his voice. "But you have to pick your battles. Instead of asking the outfitter what the guy was wearing, where on the creek it happened, then asking the same questions to the guide, I let it go. You can piss people off by riding them too hard." The approach couldn't be more different than Bob Jackson's. Indeed, Cavan says Bob's a great help to him in a good cop/bad cop kind of way. "All I have to say to some outfitter is 'well, I'm not going to be a Bob Jackson with you on this,' and right away things turn." Still, he says he gives everyone a single "get out of jail free card," and then the next time it's a citation.

It's worth noting that like a lot of other Forest Service rangers—even, believe it or not, like Bob Jackson—neither Jason nor Cavan think more law enforcement is the answer to every problem on the Teton Wilderness. They may be happy to write tickets for salting, for example, but feel the real change will come only through hunters becoming educated—that in the end clients will do what the agencies won't. Cavan talks about the remarkable improvement in compliance with no-trace camping practices among outfitters, which he credits mostly to education. "It took 15 years," he says, "but back here 15 years is nothing."

The trail crews in a given wilderness are so valuable because they're among the few people in the Forest Service who spend time on the ground. Although even the best supervisors, including Teton Wilderness manager Rob St. John, may want desperately to get out on the trail, they do so only with great difficulty, largely because they're buried under mountains of paperwork. For them as well as for the public, workers like Cavan and Jason, Dustin, Lori, and

Darren and Kate are a godsend, willing to pull monster shifts for crappy pay for no other reason than that they love being out here. Of course, some full-timers could care less who's out here in the woods, treating a district-level job as nothing more than a stepping-stone to the supervisor's office or, better yet, regional headquarters. They're the dangerous ones, everyone tells me, prone to slashing budgets just to prove how much of a tightwad they can be, all the while letting the resource go to hell. Sadly, these are also the people who often make it to the top. Which, of course, means they're the ones making key decisions about what, if anything, becomes a priority issue on national forestland.

Such indifference is a far cry from the guys who first wore the big hats around here. Ranger Rudolph "Rosie" Rosencrans for one, the man who patrolled this country through much of the first half of the 20th century. Born the son of a forester in a small village in Austria, Rosie knew even as a young boy that he was bound to cross the big water and ride into that exotic land called Wyoming—a spark lit on a family holiday in Vienna, when the Rosencrans family happened to catch Buffalo Bill Cody's Wild West show. The short of it is that Rosie was one of those kids who couldn't wipe the dreams off his shoes. When it came time to sign up for his obligatory hitch in the military he chose the navy, figuring it would afford him the best chance of landing in America. And so it happened that when his ship the *Princess Elizabeth* finally put into port in San Francisco, having made calls from China to the South Seas, Rosie left the sailor's life and headed, at last, to the Rocky Mountains.

Rosie Rosencrans, much like Cavan and company, could work like a mule. One year while he was employed at a ranch along Wyoming's Green River, a blizzard marooned a large herd of cattle. Figuring the only chance to save them was to round up help and build a trail to the animals, Rosie strapped on his skis and headed out to gather neighbors, schussing through a blizzard for 27 hours straight, covering a whopping 82 miles. Done with that he headed right back in to the herd, meeting up with the other men he'd rounded up, wielding a shovel for hours in a desperate, though ultimately successful attempt to dig them out. Far worse than the actual work, he'd recall later, was the fact that the woman who owned the ranch never even bothered to say thanks.

From the start this was a man driven by strong notions of justice. When on his first trip to Jackson he learned his traveling partner was planning to hole up there and become a counterfeiter, a fight broke out and Rosie nearly got his head cracked with a .45; thanks to some strong talk and fast fists, though, the man finally agreed to head back where he came from and leave the town of Jackson alone. Rosie began his life as a forest ranger in 1904, signing on for the grand sum of $60 a month, two good horses, and all the necessary equipment. For much of his career it wasn't counterfeiters but poachers that pushed his buttons, sending him down the trail to chase some of the baddest bad guys in the West.

In the early 20th century one of the region's most notorious poaching bands was the Binkley-Purdy-Isabel gang—a clever, if motley crew of locals who routinely moved through Yellowstone killing elk for racks, hides, and front teeth (so-called "tusks"), which they then sold for high dollars throughout the West. Knowing full well the risk of being caught by Army scouts, who by that time were making regular patrols of the park's backcountry by hopping between snowshoe cabins, the gang preferred to do their poaching in bad weather using small caliber rifles—ones that when fired would produce a noise that carried no more than a hundred yards. (At one point Ed Binkley and the boys took that concept a step further still, fashioning crude silencers.) If it were the teeth they were after, once an elk was down the men might leave it for several days, thereby minimizing their exposure to patrols. What's more, when retrieving animal parts they often traveled with boards strapped to their boots to which they'd fastened elk feet, all in an effort to disguise their tracks. In one of their better ruses Binkley showed up one day in Judge Pierce Cunningham's chambers claiming to have run into a notorious poacher everyone was looking for. While the posse was hot on that tip, Binkley and gang were elsewhere, gathering up great heaps of wildlife booty and then making a beeline for Idaho, where they were poised to ship some $10,000 worth of hides and teeth to Los Angeles. Alas, it wasn't their day. A small dog running loose was drawn to the smell of the burlap bags; he tore one open and revealed the contents to shipping authorities.

It was due to some remarkable sleuthing by Rosie over several weeks that the federal government was finally able to link those poached hides and teeth to Yellowstone Park. Unlike the incident with the marooned cattle, when the ranch owner offered not a shred of thanks for Rosie's heroic efforts, this time there was gratitude aplenty. "No more efficient ranger ever threw a diamond hitch," gushed the semi-weekly *Pocatello Tribune,* "and a handier man on webs or skis never buckled to a long slope of gleaming snow. Stockily built, with legs like Hercules, clad in khakis, wide of shoulder, deep of chest . . . such is the man who tracked Purdy and Binkley." Other writers would characterize him as "blood brother of the grizzlies," the kind of guy who walks around "with eyes wide open as men's are who fear nothing."

One of the biggest disputes Rosie had with locals was over how ranchers were using salt for their cattle on national forest lands. Despite instructions from managers to place their salt blocks evenly across the range, thereby achieving a more equal use of the available graze, cattlemen were set on merely dumping them out along streams, as they'd been doing for decades. Rosie tried time and again to explain to ranchers that their animals would fare better under the new system, but he might as well have been talking to tree stumps. Exasperated, he finally gathered up the salt blocks, packed them onto horses, and carried them to other locations. "They found out it worked," he said years later. "That cured them." When he wasn't cajoling ranchers or nabbing poachers Rosie was digging fire lines, building cabins and even a ranger station, and, in one case, escorting a frightened elderly doctor across a swollen river with a rope tied around him, leading him to the cabin of a woman in the throes of childbirth.

One day in 1913, while out riding the ridgeline above Thorofare Creek, Rosie spotted a large party of men on the stream bank below; he decided to head down and swap greetings. To his astonishment, standing at the center of the group was an older, distinguished-looking fellow with white hair. There was no mistaking his childhood hero, Buffalo Bill Cody. Cody and his guides had been searching with no luck for a place called Blind Basin; fortunately for them Rosie knew every nook and cranny of that country, and he was only too happy to show the way. "Never have I enjoyed a trip more," Buffalo Bill said later. So thrilled was he, in fact, so grateful was he to his newfound guide that, on returning to camp, he offered Rosie a souvenir of anything he saw. To everyone's amazement the forest ranger asked for a lock of Cody's hair. It was a request that surprised even the old showman, causing him to step away for a few minutes to give the matter some serious thought. Finally Cody reached back into the thickest part of his locks, gathered a few strands and offered them to Rosie, who drew his knife and carefully cut them from his head.

Local historians say that a combination of writing journals and making detailed maps, often in poor light, along with several bad bouts of snow blindness, caused severe damage to Rosie's vision. The condition grew so bad that in his late 50s he was forced to leave the Forest Service, even though he was otherwise still strong as a mule. The old ranger would live another 42 years, eventually going completely blind, residing in a small, tree-shrouded cabin on a side street in downtown Jackson.

Mabel Lyke,
Grand Junction, Colorado

Caroline Arlen
from *Colorado Mining Stories:
Hazards, Heroics, and Humor*

*"I just hang on," says Mabel Lyke of Grand Junction, looking back
on a grueling lifetime of mining. First, she was the wife of a miner,
then an enthusiastic and pioneering one herself—a "worker," she
assures us, not a "dolly." Her matter-of-fact, heartbreaking voice
is one of many in Caroline Arlen's oral history collection.*

I was born around 1932 in Nebraska, in a tent somewhere near
Lincoln. The courthouse burnt down, so I have no birth cer-
tificate. All those records were wiped out. All I remember is that
my parents lived in a tent, and they worked a truck garden with
vegetable stalls.

I got married when I was nineteen years old. He was a long-time
coal miner. We moved up to Silverton in 1962, so he could mine the
hardrock. He worked mostly at Standard Metals. They wouldn't hire
women, so I drove a school bus. I worked in cafes. I did everything
I could. We had two sons, and at that time they were just little bitty
creatures.

In 1970 my husband went to work in a coal mine over in Redstone.
I bought an old school bus that had been converted to live in. My
sons and I moved into that and drove it from Silverton to a little town
near Redstone. Eventually we moved into a house there.

I made $100 a month driving a school bus again. There were about
seven kids in our little town. I would go pick them up and take them
down to Redstone to meet the big bus. Then I met the big bus at night,
and I'd take all the kids back home. All I had was an old little van-
type thing. It was worthless. As soon as it hit snow, I had to chain the
tires. That was practically every trip I made.

I started to buy and sell coal on the side. At first I just got some for us. But it turned out, people all around us needed coal, so I started to sell it. I had a three-quarter ton pickup then. The boys and I would go over to the Bear Coal Company in Somerset. We'd load the lump coal off the ground into the truck, and then haul it back to where we lived.

Our house burned down in 1976. We lost our dog, cats, absolutely everything. I knew these people that had the motel there in Marble. They put us up in two rooms.

Long about then, the government said the mines had to have so many lady miners per male miners. The boss at the Bear already knew me from loading up coal, so he hired me. I became the first woman coal miner at the Bear. The boss took me over to begin my shift. He told those guys, "She's never been underground before, but you've probably seen her out here loading coal."

They all said, "Yeah we have," and then this one guy said, "But some times I use awful bad language in here." His name was Bob.

I said, "It's okay, Bob. I can't understand French anyway." So they thought that was funny, and I was more or less in. When my first shift was up, they asked if I was ready to go out. I said, "No." I wanted to stay. With mining, you either love it or you hate it. I loved it! I just couldn't get enough of it.

They put me on the belt line. I worked day shifts and swing shifts. Swing shift is when you go to work at 3:00 p.m. and you get off at 11:00 p.m. They'd all find one or another reason to come around and check to see if I was doing my job. I was working as hard as anybody else, so I became one of the guys. No problem whatsoever. They knew I was in there to work. When you're a woman, you're either a "worker" or a "dolly." And I was no dolly.

When my husband got itchy pants again, he moved on to Hotchkiss to mine there. I stayed on at the Bear. I would drive back and forth from Somerset to Hotchkiss sometimes.

My youngest boy decided he wanted to be a motorcycle mechanic, so he went to Florida to do that. My older boy, Buddy, had been in Grand Junction a while, and he decided to come live with me. I would come off a day shift, and my dinner was sitting on the table. He had done the housework and the laundry. We had a fabulous time. We can be in the same room and visit with each other and not say a word. It's the same way with both boys.

I was the only woman in the Bear for most of the entire time I was there. They did bring in another lady, one time, and put me to training her. I remember she told me, "I'm not looking for a friend. I have friends. I'm in it for the big bucks."

I said, "Them bucks are gonna come awful hard," but I trained her the best I could. Well, soon she was crying on my shirttail. Oh, it was too dark, and she was scared of the dark. Oh, it was too hard labor, and she was tired. I didn't have much sympathy for her, but I tried to treat her just like people.

Shortly after she came, I wound up with female troubles. I started to hemorrhage. It wouldn't quit, so I finally went to the hospital. I wound up having major surgery. When I went back to work, the other lady had already quit.

I bid for a buggy operator job in there and got it. Then they had a breakdown up at the face, where they actually mine the coal. When they had this breakdown, they stopped mining; so they put me back on the belt line. That made me mad because, damn it, I had gotten off that belt line. I thought, "Let me help you up at the face!"

I let my temper get the best of me. I was shoveling stuff onto the belt—rocks and coal. This huge piece of rock fell off the belt. I grabbed it and tore my self loose inside. I wasn't strong enough yet from the surgery. I stuck with that damn rock, because I was so mad, and finally got it back on the belt; but that was the end of me, right there. I had to take a leave of absence. I never did get back on for the Bear.

Eventually I got on for Northern Coal, and I worked there until they shut down. There were no more coal orders. I tried to get back on somewhere else. I went clear up into Wyoming, but they were full up and didn't need anybody.

I would have done anything to go back underground and mine coal. It was probably the hardest job I ever had. It was black, and it was dirty; but I liked it down there. I was used to manual labor; and, here, the money was super good, and I had insurance. I thought that was a good deal.

In 1982 I was in a car accident. I got sideswiped, and it wrecked my neck. I took up carving rock, making little animals and such. My boys talked me into selling them at the various Mountain Man Rendezvous in Silverton and wherever. I told the boys, "I'll go, but I ain't wearing no dress. I don't wear a dress for nobody. If I can wear the leather pants and leather shirts like the men, I'll do it." So I made a leather pants outfit and started selling my carved rocks at the Rendezvous.

When I finally settled with the insurance company about the car accident, I bought my little house in Grand Junction. It rocks some and the windows breathe, but I had a house.

My husband and I separated. He hadn't quite moved out when I had a stroke. The stroke kind of sliced me in half, took my whole left side away. Now I'll be talking, and I'll just draw a blank. My left hand is really giving me static. I can't hold the stone to carve my animals. So my ex-husband stayed, as my roommate. He does lots of things around here, that I can't quite make work. Mop the floors and stuff. He earns his keep.

My oldest boy and his wife gave me their old computer. I run the keyboard with my right thumb, which works really great. I've always been independent. Took care of me and a dozen others. Now I can hardly take care of me. There are days where if I went out to the shed, I couldn't find my way back home.

But I just hang on. I'm too bull-headed and determinated to let it go at that.

Alley's Miracle Ore

Andrea Peacock
from *Libby, Montana: Asbestos and the
Deadly Silence of an American Corporation*

*Work often comes with risk, but Montana-based writer Andrea
Peacock uncovers something much more sinister. This chilling
excerpt chronicles the slow recognition of something not quite right
in the heart of a small western town.*

The region surrounding the small town of Libby is an anomaly
in Montana. Enveloped by rich cedar and conifer forests, the
landscape is eerily dank and dense compared with the open,
windy country that characterizes the rest of the state. Even locals
sometimes describe their surroundings as claustrophobic. But the
humidity of the Pacific rain shadow has also made Libby a bustling
logging town for most of the last century; the climate is relatively
favorable for tree-growing, though it was the promise of minerals
under those trees that initially drew prospectors to the area in the
mid-1800s. Many had used up their luck elsewhere and ended up in
this farthest northwestern corner of Montana as a last resort. While
a few got lucky, the gold fever of these early miners rarely panned
out. It took a second mining boom starting in 1885, along with the
railroad coming through in 1892, to populate the region for good.
This time prospectors eked out a modest existence on the proceeds
of silver, lead, coal, and a smattering of gold. The economy stabilized
a bit when Wisconsin timber magnate Julius Neils took over the
sawmill, but even that work was seasonal.

The townspeople, however, saw themselves as blessed. The newspaper of those days is full of stories of gay skating parties, happy
youth playing basketball tournaments with kids from neighboring
towns, a lively intellectual community nurtured by regular Chau-
tauqua lectures brought in by the local Women's Club. There was

an occasional bar shooting or problems with bootleggers set ting up stills in the region's creeks or running whiskey from Canada. But it was quaint, harmless stuff of the sort expected in a rough-and-tumble Wild West town. The overwhelming image is of a community in love with itself, full of hardworking white men and their families acting out one of the last scenes in the greater Mani fest Destiny drama on Montana's final frontier.

It wasn't until the 1920s that Libby's second source of economic wealth was realized: vermiculite. Literally a mountain of it lay about 7 miles northeast of town as the raven flies. The ore deposit first caught the attention of Libby businessman Edward Alley during World War I, when the federal government was looking for vanadium as a source material for steel. A few oral and historical reports describe a local politician named Henry Brink showing samples of a "rotten mica"-like substance to his friend Alley, who then acquired (some say underhandedly) the mineral claim from which it came. Other accounts describe Alley poking around old mines on the mountain and accidentally setting the flame of his candle to some vermiculite ore in a tunnel wall, which popped and sizzled and expanded before his curious eyes.

A 1928 U.S. Geological Survey report characterizes the deposit as topping off the Algonkian Belt series, rock laid down prior to the Cambrian period. Geologists have dated the vermiculite and asbestos deposits at approximately 100 million years of age. The USGS surveyors describe dikes of "amphibole asbestos" up to 14 feet wide jutting through the rock. "In several places this substance composes from 50 to 75 percent of the country rock," they write. "A small amount has been mined for experimental purposes, but no commercial product is reported." The vermiculite is what really had caught their attention. The deposit was the largest known in the world: at least 100feet wide, 1,000feet long, and deeper than they could determine. "The most striking features of the vermiculite from Rainy Creek are its properties of expanding enormously when heated and at the same time assuming golden or silvery lusters. The expanded material floats on water and is nearly as light as a cork. It appears to have a very low heat conductivity and to be capable of resisting high temperature. These qualities at once suggest it to be useful for heat and cold insulation and similar purposes."

By the time of his death in 1935, Alley had turned the curious min-eral into an industry that would help support Libby nearly to the next century. But to start with, he was just a small-time entrepreneur with the soul of an inventor. His attitude gave him some thing in common with the state's indigenous people. Historian Joseph Kinsey Howard wrote in his classic book, *Montana: High, Wide and Handsome*, that the region's Indians lived as if all native plants had worth—if some-thing seemed useless, it was only be cause they had not discovered its purpose. Alley looked at his mountain of rotten mica in much the same way: there was so much of it, there had to be some use for it. He hauled samples down to his home, a pretty little ranch on the north side of the Kootenai River, and began experimenting. The ore was layered, paper-thin sheets that held water. When heated, the wa-ter turned to steam and popped the layers out. Alley built a furnace out of rock and clay on a slope so he could pour vermiculite in the top and catch the expanded rock—now light as popcorn—where it came out at the bottom. He tinkered with the temperature, firing up with waste from the sawmill, searching for the perfect balance of heat and timing. Eventually he discarded the cast-iron floor as too frail to withstand the heat, replacing it with bricks. With this setup he could turn out 4 tons of expanded vermiculite a day. He named his invention Zonolite, and used it to insulate all his own buildings, such that nearly eighty years later it still spills out, fine as silt, from loose baseboards and cracks in the walls and ceilings.

By 1924 the local paper touted Zonolite as having "a hundred and one uses." The list grew nearly as fast as Alley and, later, his team of researchers could brainstorm. Zonolite provided insulation against the cold and heat; it was easy to install and marketed as a do-it-your-self product for residential housing. It could be used in wall plaster and wallpaper, as a paint additive, as bronze printer's ink, and when mixed with plastic, in place of drywall. A Billings, Montana, company began to build floor tiling and lightweight, weatherproof roofs out of the material. Hollywood lauded Zonolite as ideal for soundproofing movie studios and enhancing theater acoustics. A fruit shipping firm announced it could save $30,000 a year per ship by insulating with Zonolite. In later years locals even came up with recipes to use a fine, powdery form of Zonolite for making bread and cookies in the hope of creating baked goods resistant to mold:

Whole Wheat Zonobread

Two pkg. dry yeast in $^1/2$ cup warm water and three cups whole wheat flour

1 $^1/2$ cups of water and three cups No.4 Vermiculite Feed Grade

1 tsp. salt

$^1/4$ cup white flour

$^1/3$ cup molasses

$^1/4$ cup sugar

At first the orders came for a carload at a time, a ton here, a couple of tons there. The first shipment by "large automobile car" was sent to a company in Hillsboro, Ohio, that manufactured office safes, bank vaults, and steel filing cabinets. The timing was good. Though some modern proponents of the mining industry would argue that there is still plenty of wealth to dig up in the area, the region's gold and silver deposits had turned out to be rather modest, and the fur trade had long been trapped out. The town's only sizable commerce before Alley's enterprise gained momentum was J. Neils's family-owned sawmill. By the mid-1920s, small shipments of Zonolite were going all over the country and beyond: Wisconsin, Nebraska, Missouri, and New Jersey, with more inquiries coming from Scotland, Japan, and London. A couple of California businessmen promised to export Zonolite to Mexico. Alley spent his spare time traveling back east, begging for investment capital to support his vision.

There were obstacles to building a world-class industry in a remote corner of Montana, and in a 1926 interview with the *Flathead Monitor* newspaper, Alley says he nearly went broke doing it. "Before Zonolite was securely established I had disposed of everything I had except a ranch and this had been mortgaged." To begin with, Alley had competitors. He didn't own the mountain, but only some of the mineral claims on it. Other miners started up their own vermiculite businesses, including the Vermiculite and Asbestos Co., the Kootenai Valley Products Co., and the Black Mica and Micalite Companies. The railroad had a virtual monopoly on transportation and could hold the region's businesses hostage with high freight rates if it chose to. But Alley had some important allies. He and Libby's mayor, Murray Gay, were from the same home town of Wilbur, Nebraska, and shared family and business matters. They were married to sisters, and in 1923 Alley sold Gay his inter est in the swank Libby Hotel (hot and cold running water "in practically every room" and the only firstclass restaurant between Spokane and Kalispell). So when Alley decided to incorporate the Zonolite Company in 1927, he naturally brought in his brother-in- law as partner. Gay served as secretary treasurer, a role he would fill until his death in 1946.

Alley also had pull at the town's daily newspaper. While some of the other fledgling companies on the mountain received occasional mentions in *The Western News,* Alley's efforts command the big headlines. When he bemoans the fact that high railroad freight costs may slow the growth of his business, a reporter immediately jumps in to avow that "if a suitable freight rate is granted, this industry will develop into very large proportions in the very near future." Three months later, the paper proclaims the "welcome news" that the Great Northern Railroad has reduced its shipping rates from $17.50 to $17 a ton for Zonolite headed to the East Coast.

Alley also persuaded the town's Commercial Club in 1925 to en dorse his operation over the other mining companies, the club prom ising "to do whatever it can to assist in any further needed financing of the enterprise." As the other mines on Vermiculite Mountain merged or collapsed, competition narrowed down to two: Alley's Zonolite Company and Bill Hillis's Universal Insulation Company. The two men were reported to be "bitter enemies," and both carried a gun when they went to their respective claims in case they saw the other. Old-timer Bob Holiday, who owned a dump truck and worked for both men, said the rivalry yielded interesting results. "The Zono lite had the best ore," Holiday re called prior to his death in 1997. "They just drove trucks into the pit and shoveled trucks full by hand. . . . On the north side, the ore was not clean, so [Universal Insulation] had to devise methods of cleaning the ore. Many methods were tried and patented. When Zonolite used all of their pure ore, they started trying methods of cleaning the ore. Every method they tried the Universal Insulation had patented."

"That may have been expensive to clear up," Holiday noted wryly. Before Alley died of a brief illness just shy of his fifty-seventh birth day in 1935, he sold the Zonolite Company to "Detroit interests," which were fronted by a man named William B. Mayo, chief engineer for the Ford Motor Company. Hillis, meanwhile, sold out to a cadre of "Chicago capitalists" whose members included Phillip and Lester Armour, of the Armour Meat Packing company. In 1939 the two former rivals merged under the name Universal Zonolite Insulation Company, referred to by locals simply as Zonolite. That's when things really started to take off.

As in Alley's day, the challenge was less to dig out and process vermiculite than to find buyers and ship it out. It was cheaper, Zonolite directors had learned, to ship the smaller, unprocessed rock than to pay for a railcar of expanded airy vermiculite. So they opened up processing plants in Minnesota, Chicago, Kansas City, Detroit, Pennsylvania, Hawaii, New York, and South Carolina, adding Cuba, Puerto Rico, India, Australia, Pakistan, Venezuela, Chile, Brazil, and Italy on the international scene. Eventually nearly three hundred such plants processed Libby ore. As of 1941, most of the vermiculite was destined to serve as "house fill," loose insulation that could be poured in between the walls. During the next decade, Zonolite gained popularity as a concrete mixer and additive for plaster. Libby vermiculite served as the "aggregate" or base material for 20 percent of the plaster manufactured in the entire country in 1949. Sales nearly doubled that year to almost $4.2million, according to a report in *The Western News,* largely be cause of the growing popularity of Terralite, a soil additive much like the vermiculite potting soil still used by gardeners today.

In short, Libby's vermiculite went everywhere.

Unlike most men who worked for Zonolite, Earl Lovick had never held a grunt's job. Yet Libby knew Earl. He was the blacksmith's son, the six-year-old boy sent to live with his mother's people in Winnipeg after his dad died. He was the young man with a college degree who came back to Libby after a stint in the army (serving in North Africa and Italy during World War II) and took the accoun-tant's job in 1948. He progressed through the ranks, steady as they come: assistant manager, general manager, and man ager of administration, staying on after Zonolite was sold to the multinational W.R. Grace & Company in 1963. During his four decades at the mine, he became Citizen Earl, serving on the hospital and bank boards; presiding over the Lions Club, Chamber of Commerce, and school board; counting the town's newspaper editor, money men, and politicians among his friends. He could open any door with a phone call and must have wielded his power judiciously: by all accounts, the man was well liked. When Zonolite started leasing a piece of land by the river to the Little League for $1 a year, Lovick was chosen to hit the first pitch at the ball field's dedication. In 1964 the local Jaycees named him "Boss of the Year." After he retired in 1983, Lovick continued to act as a paid consultant to the company. To Libby he was the face of Grace.

But when Earl died in 1998, he left behind a few close friends who prefer not to talk about him with strangers, others who will say only that Earl was popular. His widow, his second wife, Bonnie, has so far shunned the media—which could have something to do with the fact that asbestos plaintiffs started naming her husband's estate as a defendant in Earl's absence. And then there are those—lots of people—who thought they knew Earl, who now say while shaking their heads, "He seemed like a good man." Because the truth is, Earl Lovick knew that Zonolite was laced with asbestos, that Alley's miracle ore was killing miners and maybe even other townspeople. And he did nothing to warn them.

From the beginning, mining Zonolite was an experiment. Nearly all the equipment, machinery, and processes had to be designed from scratch or borrowed from other industries and modified. By the time Lovick took the assistant manager's position in 1954, the process was pretty well set in place. The men strip-mined, digging around on the surface of the mountain from the bottom up, eventually lowering the elevation on the 400-acre site by 100 feet. They used huge power shovels to carve out steep stair like benches, 28 feet tall, into the side of the hill. Big Euclid dump trucks, called "Eucs," could handle three shovel loads of rock per trip, dumping waste into Carney Creek and ore onto a conveyor belt at the trans fer point. From there, rock, vermiculite, asbestos, and all were conveyed to a series of silos, separated by grade. The ore was run through a wet mill, a dry mill, then trucked down either to a storage facility on the bank of the Kootenai River, where raw vermiculite was loaded onto railcars and shipped elsewhere for processing, or to the expanding plant in town next to the baseball fields, where Zonolite employees ran it through a furnace, popping it up to full size, and bagged it for shipping.

Men worked at all of these points: greasing conveyor belt rollers, opening gates, cleaning, bagging, loading. Nearly all of it was dusty work, Earl Lovick testified during a deposition for Les Skramstad's case against Grace. And all the dust, he admitted under pointed questioning, contained asbestos. Lovick knew more about asbestos than the average person in 1959, the year Les was hired on. As part of Zonolite's management team he had access to inspection reports filed by the State of Montana that warned about high levels of asbestos in the dust at the mine. He'd read precise descriptions in these reports of the damage that would be done to a man's lungs by asbestos, and statements that those simply living near an asbestos mine could suffer respiratory damage. He knew that the form of asbestos at Zonolite's mine was called "tremolite," that it was a straighter fiber than commercial forms of asbestos. He knew, point by point, the places in Zonolite's operation that leaked tremolite asbestos dust. And he knew that more than a third of the mine's employees were having lung problems.

Lovick testified that he believed the workers who had abnormal lung X rays must have come to the company in that condition. Local doctors—one surgeon, the rest general practitioners, none with pulmonary expertise—could not conclusively link lung problems at the mine to the asbestos, and Lovick took their word as authoritative. The miners were provided with respirators, and they should have worn them. "We believed if they wore the respirators they would be breathing air which was within the allowable concentration range," he testified in 1997. Earlier, when lawyers asked him if he or anyone else at Zonolite had told the workers exactly why wearing respirators was so important, he said no. "There are some things that [there] shouldn't be a need to explain. You shouldn't have to tell an employee that they shouldn't put their fingers to a piece of red hot iron, either, but we never told them that." This applied, too, to the kids who were caught playing in the waste vermiculite piles by the baseball fields. "We were not successful in keeping them away," Lovick said, his unspoken conclusion being that if people didn't do what they were told, they brought misfortune upon themselves.

As for the studies showing that asbestos could be harmful to people living nearby, Lovick claimed he neither worried about nor warned Libby residents because those reports dealt with commercial asbestos facilities, not vermiculite mines with asbestos contamination. When Grace purchased Zonolite in 1963, Lovick retained his job, as did all the managers at the mine. In retrospect Lovick insisted that Zonolite managers did everything practical to follow measures recommended by the state inspector for cleaning up the company's dust problem, before and after the change in ownership. They oiled the road to keep dust down, tested and rejected a vacuum cleaner system, installed new fans, tried to keep the milling equipment well maintained, and instigated a monthly "sweep down" of the dry mill.

Lovick served on a safety committee formed by Zonolite, which included both management and workers. "[They] would do an inspection each month of the operations, and anything that they deemed to be unsafe they would record and turn into management for correction, if possible," he said. That did not include, however, the fact that there was asbestos in the dust. Until Grace managers began to leak out the word "tremolite" in the late 1970s, no one on record said anything about asbestos to the employees. According to Lovick, they simply should have known. "There's every reason to think these employees were aware of it," he said. "Among other things, the union, which they all belonged to, had information on the hazards of asbestos to their welfare." But in fact, one of the mine's last two living union representatives, a feisty old man named Bob Wilkins, says he didn't find out until 1979, when he got the news from a federal health inspector and then confronted Lovick. By then, although he had told everyone who would listen, it was too late for most of the men.

As a theologian, Lutheran pastor Les Nelson has considered the question of evil in the world. It is not an idle exercise for him: Nelson's congregation includes, for instance, an extended family of forty members, thirty of whom have been diagnosed with asbestos related diseases from the mine on Vermiculite Mountain. He doesn't name Lovick directly, speaking instead of the pressures on Grace's middlemen, managers with families, needing to keep their jobs, working under pressure first from Zonolite officials in Chicago, later from W. R. Grace executives on the East Coast, to do their jobs well and to fix the dust problem without spending too much money. It is a tad uncomfortable to see things from Lovick's point of view: the

shades of gray lead Nelson and me to consider as reasonable convenient ways to minimize the asbestos problem until hundreds are dying.
Would it take someone extraordinary to do things differently?

Despite what he knew about asbestos and disease at the mine,
about the real threat to his fellow townspeople, Earl Lovick never
warned his neighbors. Maybe he was a bad man, or maybe the scope
of the impending tragedy was simply too large to accept and he lied
to himself as well as everyone else. After all, Lovick had raised his
kids here too. And he never left Libby: the man who believed his children never played in the vermiculite piles because he had told them
not to died of cancer in 1998.

Life on the Ranch

Diane Josephy Peavey
from *Bitterbrush Country:*
Living on the Edge of the Land

For the past twenty years, Diane Josephy Peavey has lived with
her husband John on their Flat Top Sheep Company Ranch in
south-central Idaho. These four short pieces capture the strong
ties of work, family, and land.

Cattle Drive

Every spring we move our cattle 50 miles across open desert, ranch
hands on horseback with dogs at their heels. We pull a cow camp for
a headquarters. The trip can take from three days with the steers to
five days with the cows and calves. We are a strange sight, a pilgrimage of sorts, of animals and men moving north for the summer to
high country, green pastures, and mild days.

The timing of the cattle drive depends entirely on feed and water
for the livestock. This year my husband and I check the route several
times. It is silent, wild lava rock and sagebrush country. The grasses
are good but lakes normally full of water are empty. It will be another drought-year crossing.

The first day of the drive, we gather the cattle at our winter head-
quarters north of Burley along the edge of the Snake River plain.
From there we begin the move north toward the snowcapped Pioneer
Mountains in the distance.

Throughout the next few days, we follow rock outcroppings,
lakes, and buttes across the desert. It is the route used by Idaho sheep
outfits for years. We all must know the trail well because the desert
is a deceptive place.

At first glance it appears to be a flat tangle of sagebrush filling
in the expanse between mountains to the north and south. But look
again. Here is a rise and fall where from a distance it appeared flat.

A lava rock outcrop pushes up from the earth burned and split open like a loaf of country black bread. Its center is hollowed like a crater, its entrance is split rimrock forming a narrow canyon.

Across the desert the pattern is repeated. A mass of rock forms a rounded butte here, a long low outcropping there—Wildhorse, Sand, Steamboat, and Wagon Buttes—rises and depressions cut into and pushed out of this complex desert landscape.

And in this illusive country, I suddenly understand how men have lost their bearings and disappeared for days. How cattle who stray from the herd are trapped in rocks and left behind. How only those who have an intimacy with the land can find the old Indian springs with cold drinking water hidden in lava rock caves. How only those who travel this country for years know its landmarks.

Yet it is not a frightening landscape. Look down at the smallest details, slow to reveal themselves. Wildflowers, pink, yellow, blue, some no bigger than a fingertip hidden among stalks of purple lark-spur and lupine. And the grass is green now, green for a whisper of time each spring, then brown too soon. Smell the sage as it fills the air with its haunting fragrance. Listen to the silence, watch the light spread across the landscape, its patterns stretching, shifting with the hours of the day. This is the Idaho desert.

The first day, we pass Steamboat Lake by midmorning, the cattle strung out in a long line. They say the area was named by a sheep-herder who reported that a heavy snowmelt filled the lake enough to float a steamboat. The story seems bittersweet as we pass the dry lakebed this drought year.

At noon, we stop at McRae Lake for sandwiches. The cattle drink from metal troughs hauled in and filled by ranch hands earlier in the day. We might camp here on the butte above this wide lake in a normal year, but today we push on, leaving behind the empty bed, kicking up dust devils in the morning wind. We accelerate our move to the high country.

The cattle string out again along the narrow road, the only trail through the east-west stretch of jagged lava rock, lustfully named the "Tetons" by old-time sheepherders. There is little sound, only faint birdsong and occasional wind brushing through the sagebrush.

Several hours later we spot the cow camp on a rise in the dis-tance. This wooden trailer, pulled each day by a pickup to our next overnight spot, is our headquarters. Inside there is a small cooking area in the front of the camp, a table and benches that pull down from the wall in the center, and bunk beds in the back of the wagon.

After supper dishes are cleared away, cowhands and friends along for the ride, sometimes as many as twelve of us altogether, gather again at the table to play or watch a little gin rummy, maybe a bet or two, with faces half-hidden in the shallow light of a lantern hung from a ceiling hook. And there are stories—lots of stories—of other crossings.

The next morning, when I start the bacon frying at 4 a.m., I hear the muffled voices of the men outside watering and saddling their horses in the dark. They come in to warm up, splash water from a tin basin on their hands and faces, then sit down under the lantern to eat. No one talks much.

By 5 a.m. we head out on horseback to round up the cattle that have wandered during the night within the several miles between the natural barriers formed by lava rock outcroppings. We are silent in the morning stillness, savoring the newness of the day, the smell of sagebrush bursting under our horses' feet.

Within an hour the air has warmed enough for us to shed our jackets and we tie them onto the back of our saddles. We may ride together for a while, two here, three there. "They're moving right out this morning," Max says. "It's going to be a hot one," he adds a little later. Then we split off again, mostly preferring the quiet of the desert. We ride far enough behind the animals not to crowd them. Later in the day the cattle will grow tired and need to be pushed, but not now. That night we camp at Wagon Butte and water the horses at the nearby Indian well.

The next day we pass Sand Flat and look north over the vast green meadows called Phildelphie Flats by the locals, now renamed Paddleford by the BLM. It is the first break in the desert and a sign the small farms of Carey are just ahead.

It is late afternoon when we cross Highway 20, the short route between Boise and Yellowstone Park. People pull their cars over to take pictures of cowboys and cattle crossing the asphalt. The world crowds in with the urgency of daily life.

We look back to the desert one last time—a place without barbed wire, without phones or people. A place of sweet-smelling sagebrush and silence broken only by birdsong. We are dusty and tired but changed by the experience, slowed by it, moved by it. It is a second home to us and every year we leave it, and springtime memories, reluctantly.

Trees

I loved the landscape of our ranch from the first moment I saw it. But I confess from the beginning I wondered if the enormous reaches of space filled with rolling hills, sagebrush, and tall grasses couldn't use just a few more trees. Of course, cottonwoods ranged up and down the banks of Friedman Creek, filtering the strong sunshine and catching the breezes to cool our cabin even on the hottest summer afternoons.

But I wondered about just a little more greenness. So I bought my husband an apple tree for our first wedding anniversary, which we planted outside our bedroom window. We watered it and waited for it to grow.

The next fall, I signed up for the Soil Conservation Service tree pro gram and the following spring collected twenty-five fragile seed-lings each just shy of a foot tall from the agency office.

I planted the tiny spruce and pine in a field along the side of the house, aspens along the dirt road to our front yard, and lilacs near the cabin doors. Then the struggle began.

For the rest of the summer I watered constantly, dragging hoses for miles from one sprout to another. I was a slave to the seedlings. I turned down lunch invitations in town, convinced the trees would die without constant watering. I cooked quick meals that fit between watering cycles. I read books, with so many interruptions to move hoses that I can't remember what the stories were about.

By midsummer I had to mark the tiny seedlings to keep them from get ting lost in the tall grasses. In October I cheered the arrival of early winter and the end of watering.

The next spring, there was no trace of the aspen twigs—gone with the snows as if they had never existed. The lilacs, spruce, and pines barely clung to life. The apple tree was even smaller than I remembered it.

I began my second summer of servitude to this project. After a flurry of spring growth that added several inches to each plant—just enough to give me a false sense of hope—the seedlings settled back to suck up the water and languish in the sun.

The cycle continued. There were losses each winter and long summer days of watering. Now, years later, only three spruces and two lilacs have survived the seasons, the drought, the ranch trucks that have backed over them, and the horses and wild game that have nibbled the tops flat. The healthiest is maybe 2 feet high, and I have lost almost all interest in them.

Only our apple tree is a triumph. After eight years it suddenly blossomed and now gives us fruit. My husband and I fawn over it.

So I gave up on my grove. And simultaneously I stopped clearing the area of cottonwood sprouts from seeds carried to the field by the winds. It was then I realized that these seedlings, without any special attention, were growing into respectable cottonwoods. Now I ponder the word indigenous. Perhaps, I reason, spruce trees would have looked a little strange in this field of tall grasses and wildness where cottonwoods have come to flourish.

Wolves

I remember clearly the day my husband rushed into the kitchen and breathlessly told me he had seen a wolf. "He was a wonderful creature," he added, and for the rest of the day it seemed his mind was far away in the fields with the wild animal again.

Several months later, our cowboy told us he had heard a wolf one morning when he was gathering the team. He had the same wonder in his voice my husband had had weeks earlier.

These events are among my husband's favorite ranch stories. "I saw a wolf here about six years ago," he'll tell visitors, "and our man heard him several months later." For him it is part of the mystery of living on the land.

Recently my husband and I went to a Wolf Recovery program at a friend's house in the city. In the enclosed yard, two long-legged, gray-brown animals on leashes strained for attention. "Get down on their level," their owner advised. "Look them in the eyes and get to know them."

We did. Smelling their animalness, looking into their glassy blue eyes, I stroked their coarse fur and wondered what it must be like to see them in the wild. I thought about my husband's brief moment with one and I envied him the experience. We told a program leader about the wolf at our ranch. The excited young man ran to tell others. Each wolf sighting is an event.

Later that evening the hosts ran a film about these animals. My husband leaned forward in his chair as if he might join them in their mountain freedom. They howled on screen once, then again, and everyone in the room became silent, stunned by the chilling sound. My husband leaned even closer to the screen.

Then the image changed in front of us. A rancher was rounding up cattle and instantly I realized that he was the bad guy. Livestock, the narrator said, crowded out wolves. Now ranchers are resisting their reemergence, afraid the wild animals will kill their sheep and cattle.

I looked at my husband. He had drawn back and sat small in his chair. And I realized suddenly that we were the enemy for people looking for simple solutions and I felt isolated in this room of friends.

Generations

I met Scott one quiet Sunday afternoon when he came to our ranch head quarters. He drove up as I was walking to my cabin and asked if he could go to the grave site of Jim Laidlaw. He told me Mr. Laidlaw had been his grandfather.

When I got back to the house, Scott and my husband were deep in conversation retelling stories Scott had heard from his mother. She was raised in this cabin. Scott sighed wistfully as he looked around the open space, brown and yellow in the warm mid-autumn day, and said, "I've never lived here but driving up the road, I know I have it in my blood."

Earlier that day I had been thinking about the three generations of families who have lived and worked on this ranch since we bought the place from the Laidlaws. My husband's grandfather, John Thomas, was first. His daughter and only child, Mary, was the second generation.

Her father pulled her aside after her husband's tragic drowning in the Snake River and told her, "Daughter, you have to learn the business and save the ranch for your son." And she did, running it until the early 1960s, when my husband, and the third generation, took over the ranch. Three generations, John Thomas, Mary, and my husband, running Flat Top Sheep Company.

Today our son, Tom, is assuming more responsibility for the ranch. He sighed one day after returning from a college friend's wedding.

"They're all making such good money," he told me. "I have to wonder if this is a mis take out here."

My heart seemed to stop when I heard him. It is a fear so many of us in agriculture know today—this tension between a love of our work and the land, and the realization that our children can provide better for their families in an urban job.

Last year Tom planted acres of wheat, barley, and canola seed, working late into the night, sleeping little throughout the spring. He watched over the rows of shoots as they grew to full crops, then stood by helplessly as an unexpected hailstorm and early frost destroyed most of them. Fields of crops turned bad, nothing to sell for all his work, little left but feed for the cattle. A bitter harvest.

Recently when I went to Tom's house, I saw two chairs pulled to the edge of the porch where he and his wife must have sat the night before watching the evening sun spread across the hillsides where the cattle grazed. Or perhaps they sat there in the morning with steaming cups of coffee watching the light fill up the quiet space. And I saw in those two chairs a sign of hope beyond loss, of a love of place that is greater than money, and a deep commitment that passes like a poem from one generation to the next.

4 ✺ Moving Across the Landscape

The West has long been a space of movement as well as settling in. Sometimes movement marks a kind of carelessness, but sometimes it is healthy, allowing us to build good lives and gain in understanding. The essays here offer rich meditations on a variety of migrations: grizzly bears and curious biologists, families traveling by foot and car in search of better times, sandhill cranes, and lines of descent that tie together relatives separated by time, space, and emotion.

Real Bear Clawing
the Backbone of the World

Douglas Chadwick
from *True Grizz*

This story from wildlife biologist Douglas Chadwick reveals as much about the all-too-human "participant observer" as it does about a mightily curious grizzly moving across steep mountainsides with an inscrutable agenda of its own.

I go grizzly watching most every autumn in the portion of Glacier National Park that lies east of the Continental Divide. The country is drier and more open than the Flathead watershed on the heavily forested west side, and bears are far easier to keep in view. My hikes follow a series of high, windy valleys roughed into broad troughs by past glaciation, sided with thick bands of uplifted sediments from the bottom of Precambrian seas, and capped by more sharply honed tiers that aspire to ultraviolet reaches of the sky. There is almost a full mile of vertical relief between the valley floors and the crags, and you wouldn't want to change a single feature in between. In a 1998 movie about the afterlife, I noticed some of these settings used as the backdrop for Heaven. They are surely as lovely as any place you could ever walk here on Earth.

With workable weather, constant scanning through binoculars, and some luck, I might locate as many as a dozen grizz during a day's east side hike. In the fall of 1998, the year of widespread berry crop failure, I spied bears all over the mountainsides. But they were the other kind—black bears. Adept tree climbers, black bears normally keep to forested habitats where they have a better chance of escaping enemies. Grizz, known to dine on their smaller cousins, are high on the list of threats. That made it all the more intriguing to find black bears foraging for hours on end across the open slopes where grizzlies should have been.

I'd heard a lot of reports about east side grizzlies patrolling for food at lower elevations that year, much as on the west side. Dan Carney, the bear management specialist for the Blackfeet Fish & Wildlife Department, confirmed the pattern. Most of the radio- collared grizz he kept track of had left the protected wildlands of the high country for the Blackfeet reservation and were wandering the foothills and the edge of the Great Plains. I took the daily presence of black bears on grizzly turf in Glacier as equally strong proof that the silvertips widely considered to be park bears were somewhere else.

To distinguish grizzlies from black bears, the Blackfeet spoke of the larger species as Real Bear. That's how I thought of grizz on the east side too, especially that year. These were no more park bears than they were Blackfeet bears, national forest bears, backyard bears—everybody's bears and nobody's bears. They were real bears, doing whatever they had to, wherever they needed to be, in the real world of 1998.

During the first of my trips to Glacier's east side another year—a decent one for wild fruits—I found grizzlies in their usual September haunts on the valleys' floors and lower slopes, mouths stained purple from rummaging through huckleberry and serviceberry branches. Now and then, they added buffaloberries, chokecherries, wild currants, and mountain ash berries to the mix. I returned in mid October after most of the berries were gone. Instead of trekking all over as I usually did, I spent a week watching a solitary grizzly work its way around the side of a mountain and up toward its crown.

The bear was a large, dark brown, well-fed adult with a luxuriant coat grown out in anticipation of winter. Not for another year would its fur appear so shiny and new, much less cover a midsection so round or a rump so wide, rippling with stored fat. This was a prosperous-looking bruin, portly, baronial—one big-ass bale of life force. I want to tell the tale of our meeting on top of the world.

Winter had already claimed the highest elevations. Coated with fresh crystals, the strata above 8,000 feet gleamed like bands of pure marble or chalk. The slopes below were just on the cusp, with the east side gusts sometimes slinging rain, sometimes sleet, and occasionally blizzards. Then the sun would break through to soften the snowflakes and send meltwater trickling over the cliff ledges. An hour later, the rivulets might be frozen and the ledges glassy with newborn ice while another tempest brewed.

In the beginning, the grizzly was on a south-facing talus slope toward the base of the mountain. Bighorn sheep grazed to one side. Mountain goats lay bedded among broken cliffs on the other. Preoccupied with digging for roots, the bear paid no attention as I climbed within viewing range—not close, just near enough to pick out details with a fifteen- to forty-five-power telescope. On a later day, the grizzly was going after more roots by scraping away the thin topsoil on ledges, when a herd of bighorn ewes and young crossed above. They bedded down less than 200 feet away. One ewe walked downhill to within 100 feet for a closer inspection. Though I've seen grizz chase bighorns in the Rockies and Dall's sheep in Alaska, the bear paid no more attention to that particular observer than to me hundreds of yards away.

A couple of days after that, the bear was halfway up the west facing side of the mountain. I passed a moose in a brush-fringed meadow and a coyote nipping off old mountain ash berries before busting my way uphill through jungles of alder and false huckleberry, or snowbrush. I hit a maze of elk trails with fresh droppings and finally followed them out of the shrub tangles onto open talus. Above, purplish red layers of the silty limestone called argillite out cropped here and there in narrow belts. Their ledges held ground-hugging juniper shrubs and scattered copses of subalpine fir scores of years old but seldom more than head high.

Terrific winds were tumbling off the Great Divide. This was the first slope they hit. Braced against them, I made for a thicket of the stunted firs and scrunched down among the tough, springy branches. Their bittersweet, turpentine scent enveloped me even in the gale. Each time the bear came within a few hundred yards, I began edging away toward another cluster of fir. More often than not, the animal would turn before I had to move, and my telescope would offer a rear-end view of featureless, wind-rippled fur. Only the longer hairs on the hump stood out, parting and fanning as the bear put its shoulder muscles to work.

The grizzly kept digging nonstop, unearthing roots of vetch, in the pea family, and lomatium, or biscuitroot, in the carrot family. It had been doing the same for days, raking through the talus whenever I first spotted it in the morning and when I last looked before leaving in late afternoon. Being in full hyperphagia, the prehibernation drive to put on as much fat as possible, the animal probably kept at it through much of the night. Virtually every step I took landed on part of a small crater, either freshly excavated or left from an earlier year and beginning to fill in with scree.

Scalloped by grizzly claws and dotted with grizzly droppings, much of the upper mountainside was loose and slidey, still seeking its angle of repose. The big sky was more than unsettled; it was hyper, reminding me of speeded-up movie scenes in which storms seem to gather and fade within moments. Migrating golden eagles shot through unraveling clouds, while swaths of sunlight and shadow raced one other across faraway slopes turned burgundy and gold. All this motion was framed by massive vaults of stone more than a billion years old, standing unperturbed, anchored in geologic time. Here was the realm the Blackfeet knew as the Backbone of the World.

The morning dawned bright when I began bushwhacking uphill with some companions on a different day, toward the end of the week. By the time I emerged from the snowbrush, clouds were piling up against the west side of the divide. They darkened and swelled at an impressive rate, chafing against the highest peaks. Yet the forward edge of the storm stayed brilliantly lit by strong sunlight from the east. Inner whorls flickered and glowed. A shimmering nimbus spread around the edges, and luminous streaks of vapor flared outward from that into the blue. If trumpeting archangels had paraded from this gloriole, you would have nodded and said, "Of course." Not to overdo the analogy, but as you ascend toward the upper limit of the life zone, you can't escape some of the feeling of having cast off earthly things to stand unadorned before powers far greater than your own. Add a grizzly, and the notion is entirely justified.

Real Bear, as I had come to think of this particular grizz, was higher and farther toward the head of the valley than on any day before. While I huffed that direction, the storm slipped its mountain top moorings and began to surge east. The nearer you draw to the base of rock outcrops, the more thoroughly they screen the landscape above. I was thinking that Real Bear was still a considerable distance away and more to the north, when the animal abruptly appeared at the outer edge of a ledge looking straight downhill at me through a stinging rain.

It was a fixed stare, and grizzlies have better vision than many credit them with. Even so, I couldn't be sure whether Real Bear truly had me in view or was orienting partly by smell. I didn't think I was anywhere near close enough to be considered a threat, so I stopped and waited. Real Bear leaned forward, sifting the wind with flared nostrils, then sat on its rump and slowly waved its massive head back and forth.

Through binoculars, I looked for any sign of agitation or alarm. But the ears weren't laid back, the muzzle stayed smooth, the eyes soft. Real Bear seemed concerned only with testing the air more thoroughly. I wasn't too worried that catching my scent at that distance would spur the grizzly to react strongly one way or the other. Busy park trails intersected the berry patches and other prime habitats that the bears frequented on lower slopes earlier in the year, and most of the grizz hereabouts were somewhat conditioned to the scents and sounds of humans as a result. Every year or two, news papers trumpet the news: Hiker Mauled in Glacier Park. Never once will they headline the truly astounding annual event that I would rather see publicized: 100,000-Plus Hikers with Varying Levels of Skill and Intelligence Bumble through Glacier's Grizzly Country Unscathed.

Real Bear lay down facing my direction with its chin atop crossed paws. I dropped away downhill and moved farther toward the head of the valley. My plan was to negotiate a separate, taller section of the cliff belt. But the climb began to turn more and more iffy, and I couldn't be sure of where I would top out in relation to the grizzly if it moved. So I retraced my steps, making a wide swing down the valley to get around the ledge where Real Bear had been, until I could see the animal again. From there, I proceeded to scramble up another third of the mountainside. Perched nearly a quarter of a mile above, I could keep track of the bear now without it disappearing behind breaks among the cliffs or into the swales and runoff channels creasing the talus fields.

At the time, I considered my position to be comfortable from the standpoint of safety and poor only in terms of shelter. There was none. I was surrounded by sparse, low vegetation, rock debris, and grizzly-dug craters. The weather, already nasty, was deteriorating. With a foot in one pawed pit, I kicked with my other boot at the rubble heaped around it, trying to fashion a level shelf on which to stand.

The wind kept flinging sleet sideways into my face. My boots were proving to have too many miles worn through the layers that were supposed to keep them water-resistant. I was damp and cold, and the gale made my eyes water, blurring my vision. Then it started to snow. And then I wasn't comfortable from the standpoint of safety either, because the bear had been slowly, barely noticeably, yet steadily, zigzagging uphill toward my spot.

The white squalls came in waves with stripes of sun dazzle between them, washing over thousands of vertical feet of rock walls in the background, over turquoise lakes pooled at their feet, over blackish green forests lining the valley floors, and across the long, open slope I was on. Real Bear was a sharply outlined figure with bright cinnamon and silver highlights one moment, a shadowy mass in a blur of snowflakes the next. A mass still moving uphill. During the peak of a squall, I crept higher on the talus. The grizzly went back and forth and even turned downslope for a short distance. Then it continued in my direction.

The allure of grizz and stories about them has always been bound up with the feeling of matching skills or wits with a potentially lethal beast. Even if the animal has other concerns and you only imagine that a matchup is happening, you face questions about the stuff you're made of. The person you liked to think you were just moments before, the things you held dear all those earlier days, the wisdom of your long-term goals—these are subjects suddenly up for review. And you may discover that what you want out of life above anything else, and what you would settle for, and what you never quite appreciated for the gift that it is, is to remain alive. Anything more counts as accessorizing.

What Real Bear would have made of my thoughts or what its intentions were, I couldn't say. The grizzly seemed careful to avoid looking directly my way as it neared. It was not terrifyingly close, and it was still absorbed in digging. On the other hand, I was three-quarters of the way up that mountain, so exposed on the slope and so far from escape cover that I was out of options and simply stood there tingling from my scalp to my marrow as though I had just seen the stars at midday. It was up to Real Bear now.

Water trickled off icicles on the sides of boulders. More water flowed under the ice encasing flat rocks, and the air bubbles squeezing between the stone and the crystal panes made wobbly abstractions. I remember gazing at them completely entranced. It could have been a trick of the mind to give itself a break. Or maybe my circuitry temporarily jammed. A beam of sunshine swept across a distant limestone palisade like a searchlight. The grizzly glanced at me out of the corner of its eye but kept its head down, feeding.

To warm my toes, I shifted from foot to foot, but smoothly so as not to make any attention-getting lurch. I listened to the sound of blood pulsing in my ears. Dried sulfurflower stalks shivered in the wind and loosed the snow gathered on their small umbels. Real Bear shook the moisture off its coat and glanced at me again. When it turned to feed along a different tangent, quartering away, I walked slowly in the other direction, stepping from crater to crater, one eye on my footing, the other on the grizzly.

Real Bear kept digging. Speeding up my pace, I went farther to the side and started angling downslope. I dropped over a ledge and landed on a fresh set of excavations—deep ones, probably to unearth ground squirrels, judging from the intact burrows around. I kept going. When, at last, I paused for a long look back, Real Bear merely had its nose down in a new pit.

My thoughts had progressed from "Please, bear" to "Thank you, bear" to "Damn, this must be the hardest-working grizz in the getting-fat business." And it could scarcely be going about its labors farther from people, their homes, or any kind of trouble, I reminded myself. The problem animal here, the one pushing the boundaries of acceptable behavior, has two legs. My legs. The bear, and only the bear, conducted itself honorably the whole time.

An hour later, I finally hit the forest toward the valley bottom and walked out of the drainage, and that was it for grizz-watching in the tall country that year. The next year, I went back and found Real Bear, or its twin. Same size, same color, same place, digging away. As before, I was hard put to find a section of the slope that hadn't been altered by grizzly toil. Real Bear was single-pawedly tearing the face off a mountain.

Given the sheer numbers of hoary marmots, golden-mantled ground squirrels, Columbian ground squirrels, pocket mice, and voles in the high country, you would expect these ubiquitous burrowers to be the primary earth movers there. Yet according to a recent study in Glacier

Park, silvertips shift more soil than any other wildlife in the alpine and subalpine zones. One of the reasons grizzlies turn over so much ground is to get at all the aforementioned rodents, especially those hibernating when the bears are not. For the most part, though, the big omnivores are hunting the nutrients stored in plant roots and bulbs.

Grizz scarify and disturb countless acres this way in the short run. Over time, they end up fashioning richer, more varied plant communities. Raking and plowing swaths across a landscape, the bears loose countless seeds and spread them around. They also plant them in improved soil, because all that excavating brings scarce nitrogen from lower ground levels to the surface, the result farmers seek when they till their fields. This fertilizing effect causes vegetation such as glacier lilies and spring beauties to grow more vigorously and produce more seeds than they do in undisturbed sites. Though it is hardly part of their public persona, grizzlies are, in effect, big-time wildflower gardeners.

You'll find similar grizzly-modified habitats down low on riverbanks and gravel bars, where the search for the starchy roots of a vetch called *Hedysarum* leaves the ground contoured like a practice range for small mortars. In Alaska, I found stretches of Brooks Range tundra reworked by grizz into that same oversize egg carton pattern for miles along well-drained hillsides and old moraines. Dan Carney showed me where grizzlies had been digging in rangelands out on the high plains, mainly for roots but also to get into the brood chambers of hornets that nest underground.

Nearly every grizzly that Carney radio-tags and follows dens high on Glacier's snow-buried mountainsides. Upon awakening months later, a large percentage exits the park for the early green-up lower down. Keeping close to woodland groves and streamside brush for cover when near human territory, some stay on while spring gives way to summer. Others move back into the park as soon as the melt starts up the big valleys.

Around midsummer, a number of grizzlies continue upward all the way to the peaks. They are after army cutworm moths, which migrate from the prairies to spend the warm months close to the very crest of the Continental Divide. The insects sip nectar from alpine flower fields (partly cultivated by grizz) through the night, pollinating blossoms as they go. By day, they shelter beneath rock rubble, congregating on certain talus slopes or boulder fields in astronomical numbers. The moths stay until early fall, and a good many grizzlies stick with them, overturning stones to lick up the diminutive prey.

When the moths first arrive in the high country, their bodies are about 40 percent fat. By fall, they have abdomens plump as jelly beans from weeks of lapping plant sugars and are closer to three quarters fat. That makes them the richest source of energy a grizzly can tap in the ecosystem. Pound for pound, these winged nougats provide more calories than roots, berries, nuts, or, for that matter, straight red meat.

Although biologists have counted as many as two dozen grizzlies feeding together on moths in a single talus field, the number of such insect lodes is limited. Once berries begin to ripen in mid-August, fruit becomes the most widespread and abundant of all bear meals in this stretch of the Rockies. By late September, that bounty is fading, the moths are leaving to overwinter on the Great Plains, and some bears abandon the park again to forage down in the foothills and beyond, only to turn around with the coming of winter and journey to the reserve's lofty slopes to sleep.

In light of all the back-and-forth movement, this population never really qualified as park bears. There were individuals that spent a great deal of time inside the protected part of the ecosystem, and individuals that spent less. Before grizzlies were safeguarded under the Endangered Species Act, those that went beyond the sanctuary simply kept getting picked off. The deaths were not always reported; bears just disappeared. If you went to count grizz, you found so few outside the reserve that it looked as though the bears strongly favored park lands. Thus, when officials first sketched out what they considered to be habitat essential to grizzly recovery, they drew the eastern limit right along Glacier's eastern boundary.

Carney told me, "After a few years, we looked over our locations for radioed bears and realized we'd better move the line about ten miles farther east to Highway 464. Now I've got bears roaming way east of there. One nearly made it to Cutbank [a town about forty miles outside of the park]."

Whether you're among east side cowboys, west side loggers, or Montanans in general, if the discussion turns to bears and efforts to save them, it seems that someone sooner or later asks: What good is a grizzly anyway? When I visit an animal like Real Bear along the Backbone of the World, the setting is so charged with wild beauty, the experience so strong and unalloyed, that it never fails to answer the question. Grizz strengthen the spirit. They create wonder. They humble. They temper. They clarify and awaken. They do me a world of good.

I don't recall observing a grizzly that looked like Real Bear on the park's east side during the bad berry year of 1998. Haphazard as my surveys are, the animal could easily have been around. I probably overlooked it or else didn't recognize it. Then again, it could well have been out on national forest, tribal, or private lands with the other grizz. It probably visited nonpark sites every year at some point before returning to the mountainside in Glacier where I observed it digging day after day.

So even as I am watching real bears walk close to the heavens, having myself a pure nature binge and romanticizing away, I try to keep in mind that the lives of these same animals depend from time to time upon what goes on in the less perfect, more worldly dimensions of the ecosystem. Grizz will recover only to the extent that we guarantee them some room there beside us.

Tumbleweeds

Mary Taylor Young
from *Land of Grass and Sky:
A Naturalist's Prairie Journey*

*Mary Taylor Young relates a Dust Bowl era story from her mother,
combining history and personal recollection to make the natural
world more vital and understandable.*

I walk through brittle grass in late summer along open fields
northeast of Denver, grasshoppers leaping ahead of me, spring-
loaded. They ricochet at odd angles, colliding with my bare legs,
scratching me with whiskery feet. Fallen to the ground, the 'hoppers
laboriously gather their backward-bending legs beneath them and leap
off again. Grasshoppers seem born of drought, speckling the grassland
like surrogates for the drops of rain that haven't fallen. Today, like yes-
terday and the day before, the land and air are hot and dry. Scant rain
has fallen this summer. I pass wide farm fields of bare dirt plowed into
furrows, other expanses broken by earthmovers preparing an invasion
of tract homes. The wire fences bordering these acreages are heaped
with breastworks of dirt and tumble weeds piled up like pennies pitched
against an alley wall. There's a strange symmetry to these slopes, which
rise always on the west side of the fences. Wind following the work of
the plow and the bulldozer has carved these mounds. The scene seems
strangely familiar, though I know it only from old photographs dating
from the 1930s and from my mother's stories.

"It was Dust Bowl days then." That's how Mom always begins
her stories about her journeys as a young girl in the 1930s across the
eroded deserts that had been the wheat fields of western Kansas and
eastern Colorado. She was little Patty then, about 12 years old, with
two big brothers—Bert and Bob—and a baby sister, Emma Jean.
Mom grew up in eastern Kansas, not on the dry prairie, but along the
wooded, hilly banks of the Missouri River where flood is a more fear-

some foe than drought. That part of Kansas at the edge of the prairie, with its hills and stands of native trees, feels more like the East than the West. To escape the hot, humid weather, my grandparents began the family tradition of spending a few weeks each summer in the cool air high in the Rocky Mountains. In 1934, Granddad left his Chevrolet dealership in the hands of a manager and drove the family on the first of many road trips to Estes Park, a cross-prairie migration that survived into my childhood. But between the Missouri River and the Rocky Mountains lay 600 miles of the hot and dry, then the heart of the Dust Bowl. The images from those trips are burned so vividly on my mother's memory that even after more than 60 years, she relates her stories in great detail.

I've heard the stories before, but I have a new interest in this time when the prairie, like an angry, wounded bear, turned on the people who had been such poor stewards of the land. "Tell me what it was like during the Dust Bowl," I ask her.

"It all started with the long drouth," Mom explains. She always pronounces the word drought with a "th" in the Midwestern fashion. The newspapers of the time, of course, were full of the devastating dry-up of western Kansas, the failure of crops, the blowing clouds of topsoil. My grandparents planned the trips west carefully, figuring on a two-day hard pull to get to the mountains, with one overnight stop midway. The family road trips when I was a kid were long and dull, but we were always sure of finding places to buy gas and food. Not so in the 1930s, when travelling across the Dust Bowl was a serious undertaking. In those days, there were no McDonalds where families could stop for a quick hamburger. Knowing provisions might be hard to find along the way, my grandmother packed big jugs of water and baskets of food to carry with them. They held the sandwiches, fruit, and cookies that make a road trip more bearable. As usual, Patty was squeezed in the backseat between her two big brothers, while Emma Jean, the baby, sat between my grandparents in the front seat. No one was comfortable, of course, since August on the prairie is mercilessly hot, drought or otherwise. Car packed, people and vehicle fed and watered, the family pulled out of Leavenworth and away from the Missouri River.

Rolling along through the shadeless open country, their car became a convection oven, baking the family inside like a batch of powder biscuits. There was no air conditioning in those days, so they had the windows rolled down, since a dry breeze was better than being closed up in the stifling car. The sun burned bare arms leaning on the window sills. Dust blew in the windows, coating sweaty bodies with grit. My grandmother wet towels and draped them across the open windows trying to cool the air by evaporation, but it didn't work very well.

Granddad was a formal man. Even on vacation in the mountains he wore a starched shirt, creased trousers, and wingtip shoes. But that prairie heat forced him to relent. Gone were his usual coat and tie. The sleeves of his white shirt were rolled up above the elbows. It was the only time Mom remembers seeing her father dressed so casually. The family headed west along two-lane highways that today still bear the same number designations as they did 60 years ago, US Highways 24 and 40. Their Chevrolet sedan, a big boxy car with sturdy fenders and a big engine, motored along like some great, dark beetle crawling over the dun-colored plains. In those days most cars were painted in dark colors—black or navy blue—which only made them hotter inside. The interstate highway system didn't exist yet but in that wide open country, speed limits didn't mean much anyway. "My dad drove way over the speed limit out there most of the time," Mom says with a conspiratorial smile as if tattling on her father.

The road was lonely. Theirs was usually the only car on the highway and meeting another vehicle was an event. They'd watch its approach from a long way off, appearing as a speck trailing a plume of dust, then growing larger and larger. The boys, both enthralled with cars, tried to be the first to guess what model of car it was. With not much to do to pass the time on the long trip, they played cards and word games—I am Annie from Atlanta and I'm carrying an apple, I'm Bert from Baltimore and I've got a baseball. "My mother was a real bee on those word games," Mom remembers with a laugh. Singing songs was good for burning up the miles. They sang lots of folk songs like *Rolling On The River,* and silly pop tunes of the day like *The Flat Foot Floogie.* "The Ding-Dong Daddy song?" I ask hopefully. "I don't remember that one till a lot later," Mom says with a smile.

Despite their diversions, the emptiness of the land was oppressive. It wasn't just the sameness of the open landscape, which would bore my sisters and me in later decades, but the deadness of the miles and miles of abandoned farmland without a hint of life that wore down their spirits. Humans need the affirmation of life around them, but in that desolate country there was no wheat or corn growing in the fields, no grasses or wildflowers, not even a coyote or jackrabbit or meadowlark.

"The worst part was the ghost towns," Mom remembers. Many towns along the highway were empty, the inhabitants gone, fled perhaps to California, like the Joads in Steinbeck's *Grapes of Wrath*, but just as likely to somewhere else in the Midwest. Entire towns, which a few years earlier had been bustling farm communities, were completely abandoned. These collections of empty buildings were eerie and disheartening to the young family driving into them, reinforcing their sense of being the only living things in a land of the dead. The feeling that someone had been in these towns before her, leaving behind traces of their lives and a bit of their spirits, was very strong to Mom, a feeling she has never forgotten.

As they approached a town, Granddad would slow the car, never knowing if this place was still inhabited or had been left to the wind. The whole family, their anxious faces peering out the open windows, searched hopefully for signs of life. They would have welcomed the sight of a weary farmer, or even a scrawny dog. But town after town held nothing except empty frame houses, worn out and peeling, their shutters banging in a ceaseless, dry wind. The wind was everywhere, whispering a constant shhh. Mounds of dirt sloped against the houses in drifts like the fallen snow of a brown blizzard. The hurly-burly rolling of tumbleweeds replaced the motion of living things, blowing up against buildings and catching in fence lines, their round, skeletal bodies piling up like the ghastly remains of a holocaust. There were no crops in the fields, just drifting rows of dirt. Curtains of dust blew incessantly, carried by a wind that never stopped. Here and there amid the fields of dust stood forlorn farmhouses and barns, all abandoned. Only ghosts walked among those fields and homes.

The family motored through this devastated landscape like odd tourists in a surreal world. The emotional impact aside, there were some real concerns over making it through. Like twentieth-century pioneers, they headed off across the plains never knowing where they might find an outpost offering supplies. Finding gas was a concern and when they came to a town with an open filling station, Granddad would pull in and fill up, even if the tank was only down five gallons. The towns that still had occupants and offered a few services posted warning signs that underscored the desolation of the country—"No Gas for 100 miles." The men at those gas stations looked gaunt, dried-up, and dusty. Granddad always chatted with them for a while, asking what was up ahead, inquiring about how things were going, whether many people had given up and left, commiserating over the lack of rain. Sometimes the station owners seemed exhausted by it all, but often they had a survivor's wry outlook: "The land already blew five states over so if we hang on long enough it'll blow back around to us." In one town some jokester had put up a handlettered sign—"Land For Sale, Cheap" with an arrow pointing up to the sky.

The kids used the gas stops for a chance to go to the bathroom and stretch their legs. Nana refilled the water jugs and bought cold Coca Colas for everyone, and sometimes candy, though never candy bars, which would melt to a chocolate mess in the heat. Patty liked the chance to step inside out of the sun, which beat down mercilessly without a cloud to offer relief. Entering a small filling station in one town whose name she has long forgotten, its once-white walls battered to weathered gray, she stood blinded for a moment after the glare outside. As her vision adjusted to the dark interior, she saw a boy about her own age sitting on a stool by the cash register, watching her. The boy wore tattered overalls and scuffed shoes, and his dark, straight hair was blunt cut at the level of his chin. With a start Patty realized the boy was really a girl, and she looked grimy all over, covered with a coat of dust. While Patty's own clothes were soiled from the trip, her white blouse and plaid skirt still looked new, her brown leather shoes had the sheen of a polish, and her dark hair was clean, brushed and clasped on the side by a barrette. Patty felt embarrassed at her own good grooming and for the other girl, who looked like a ragged, dirty boy. But the girl didn't seem conscious of her scruffy appearance. Her face brightened at sight of another her own age. "Where you heading?" she asked in a friendly voice, and Patty felt ashamed of her judgment of the girl.

"To Colorado," Patty said, "to the mountains."

The girl grinned. "I'd sure like to go there. We never been but I've seen pictures and it's cool and blue and clean there."

Patty didn't know what to say. She felt suddenly sad for this bright-eyed girl trapped in this dreary brown place who dreamed of a land that was cool and blue and clean.

The big Chevy was a workhorse of a car, holding up admirably under the extreme conditions. Since Granddad was a cautious man, they never ran out of gas in all of their trips, but occasionally the heat got the better of the car. When it overheated, Granddad would pull over to the side of the road and carefully raise the hood to avoid being scalded by steam. When the radiator had cooled, he'd carefully refill it with some of their precious water.

One year the family had made it across Kansas and over the state line into Colorado. As they approached the town of Burlington from the east, my grandfather glanced to the southwest and saw something dark and ominous heading toward them. The swirling, boiling ghost of a dust storm was on a collision course with the car. Everyone living in the Midwest had heard the horror stories about the dust clouds. Cattle out on the range with no cover when the dust storms blew in were found drifted over, suffocated by dust. People caught outdoors by one of these dust clouds were in real danger of being engulfed and smothered. Even indoors the fine dust found its way through tiny cracks and crevices, under doors, down chimneys and around windows. Dust-caused asthma and pneumonia sickened people and many children would die of respiratory problems before the "Dirty Thirties" were over.

"We've got to beat this storm to Burlington," Granddad told my grandmother in a low voice. Her face grew taut and pale. She glanced over her shoulder at her children in the backseat. The whole family, even little Emma Jean, fell silent, knowing the gravity of the situation. The only sound was the rhythmic drone of the tires and the increasing roar of the wind.

As if trapped in a Jungian nightmare, chased by a dark cloud of doom, Granddad floored the gas pedal, whipping the Chevy like a team of horses in a neck-and-neck race with the storm. Face grim, head bent over the wheel, shirtsleeves rolled up, sweat making his skin stick to his back and shoulders, Granddad piloted his Chevy in a sprint for safety. The car barreled along, the storm loomed closer.

Finally the grain elevators of Burlington came into view. "When we get there, you kids don't stop for anything, you just run inside as fast as you can," my grandfather said sternly. They pulled up at the little hotel. The day had gone dark, the cloud was almost on them. Without pausing to grab their luggage the family jumped from the car and dashed for the hotel just as the dust descended. The hotel owner and her daughter had seen them pull up and were waiting at the front door like guards at the castle gate. As the family reached the door the two women threw it open just long enough to let the frantic arrivals dart through, then slammed it shut behind them as the dust storm hit. Driven by the wind, the pitiless din pelted the building, rattling against its frame sides like hail. The hotel owner passed out damp towels for the family to hold over their faces to keep from choking as the air in the room filled with powdery dust, sifting in through the cracks despite wet rags stuffed around windows and under doors. Holding the moist cloth to her face, Patty walked with her mother into the living room that also functioned as a lobby. A handful of people sitting and standing around the small room with their faces obscured by towels looked like a strange tribe of desert people. They regarded each other silently with eyes that were tired and fearful. Some covered their faces completely with the towels. Nobody spoke. The room was eerily silent of voices but loud with the pattering racket of the dust storm. It was only about 5 p.m. on an August afternoon, but the day had turned as dark as dusk as the dust filled the air and blotted out the sun. The dim glow of candles offered the only light; the electricity had been knocked out by the wind.

The hotel proprietor managed to make sandwiches to serve everyone for dinner, buttering the bread, adding the meat and cheese, then slicing the sandwiches all by feel because she had covered the food with dish towels to keep out the dirt. The dining table where the small group of guests ate together family style was covered with a thick film of fine dust. There wasn't much dinner conversation, just coughs and sneezes. Sitting at the table eating her sandwich beneath a cloth tied around her face like a stagecoach bandit, Patty idly began writing her name in the dust on the tablecloth, till my grandmother, seeing what she was up to, hurriedly scolded her and wiped the spot clean. With nothing to do, bedtime came early. Nana made the children sleep with their coats tented over their faces to filter out the dust.

The next morning, residual dust from the waning storm masked the dawn and powdered the highway as if a brown snow had fallen. Continuing their journey, the family traveled through a war-ravaged land. In some towns only one building still stood; the rest had been knocked down by the wind. Granddad stuck to the paved road because many of the side roads were blocked by wind-sculpted drifts of dust. As they drove west, gradually leaving behind the devastated plains of the Dust Bowl, conditions improved. Finally, somewhere west of Limon, the Rockies shimmered into view on the horizon. They had journeyed through the maelstrom and come out the other side.

Mom and her family were only observers to the great price paid in human suffering and loss during the Dust Bowl. Many other families in Kansas, Colorado, and adjacent states were not so lucky. More than 10,000 farms were abandoned by destitute families during the Dirty Thirties. What happened to the families who had lived in those ghost houses my mother saw? I doubt there are many records of where those busted farmers ended up. Like their farms, they just blew away with the wind.

Mom, like most who lived through the Dust Bowl, has always blamed "drouth" for the cataclysm, but dry periods are an integral part of shortgrass prairie ecology. Those who study climate cycles say that the drought of the 1930s was not as severe as other dry spells the High Plains has seen in recent centuries, even in recent decades. So what happened differently to create the Dust Bowl?

Environmental historian Donald Worster, author of *Dust Bowl* and *Rivers of Empire,* has thought a lot about the causes of this ecological cataclysm. As with so many passions, there is a story behind his fascination. Worster's parents lived through the Dust Bowl in Kansas, fleeing eventually to California, where he was born.

Worster expands upon the usual suspects of drought and exhaustive farming to name agricultural capitalism—the rush to turn the Western prairies into a vast money-making grain factory with no regard for the ecological consequences—as the true culprit for the Dust Bowl. With invention of the mechanical combine, wheat could be cut and threshed in a fraction of the time needed to do the work manually. After World War I, with Europe in a shambles, the price of wheat boomed. Big dollars could be made on the fruited plains of America. The stage was set for what Worster calls the Great Plow-up. Between the mid-1920s and mid-1930s, 33million acres of virgin prairie were broken for cropland, turning under drought-resistant native grasses and leaving the soil naked to the wind. To disrupt the network of native vegetation that bound the soil and maintained the integrity of the prairie ecosystem was like crumbling a brick wall and leaving the debris in a pile. The prairie lay crumbled to dust and vulnerable. Like the Devil smelling opportunity, drought arrived, and then catastrophe.

But ultimately it was a spiritual bankruptcy, a loss of connection to the land, he says, that fomented the catastrophe. Agribusiness had emerged to replace individual land ownership. Huge corporate farms and absentee landowners replaced small family farmers, then leased the land to tenants. "In most Dust Bowl counties," writes Worster, "less than half the land was owned by residents." In Colorado's most southeastern county, Baca County, the rate of tenant farmers was only 3 percent in 1910. By 1935, it was 44 percent.

Men who owned the land no longer worked it. Acres and acres of the Great Plains were farmed by tenants who had only a tenuous emotional tie to the land and moved on frequently. Tenants lacked the personal connection of landowners, seeing the soil as a commodity to be worked hard each season, not nurtured for the future. Neither was there much love of the land in company boardrooms. The open country was no longer the cradle of family, home and culture but just one more commodity to be used for maximum profit.

A climatic drought triggered the Dust Bowl, but it was helped out by a second drought: one of heart and spirit, not water.

Finally, instead of understanding the limitations of the land and learning its rhythms, farmers tried to impose their will and their ways on a land that could not withstand the changes. Intensive farming practices used in the East were not appropriate for the shortgrass prairie. In both a physical and a metaphysical sense, the people were out of harmony with the land, upsetting the balance of the prairie ecosystem, and chaos resulted.

Is a bare and blowing prairie still a prairie? In most years, the prairie I visit grows knee-high with pale green grass in May and is studded with wildflowers of one hue or another through the summer. By autumn equinox rabbitbrush paints the land a marvelous gold. But if I ripped the hide of grass and flowers off this prairie it would be just a place. Before the Dust Bowl, the High Plains farmer had an identity, that of a tough, hard-working man of the soil, making a life in a tough land. But in the end, busted, destitute plainsmen were forced to abandon the land. The derisive term "Okies" ironically described them as the people they no longer were. When they stumbled west to California or other places, with gaunt-eyed children and meager belongings, they no longer hailed from Oklahoma or the plains states at all. They were no longer people of the land but itinerants blown away from the land along with the dust. The prairie had defined them, yet their own actions had broken that covenant. Without a relationship to the land, they were landless both physically and spiritually.

Ute Trail, Colorado

Andrew Gulliford
from *Sacred Objects and Sacred Places:
Preserving Tribal Traditions*

*Historian Andrew Gulliford's thought-provoking book sensitively
portrays the spiritual roots of Native America's relationship to the
land. In this case study, he makes vivid the fading traces of the Ute
Nation's journeys across their landscape.*

Finding intact Indian trails in the United States at the end of the
twentieth century is a major historical discovery, but thanks to
dedicated volunteers, archaeologists, and Ute Indian spiritual
leaders, one of the last pristine Indian trails left in America has been
located. Fifty-seven miles long, the Ute Trail across the Flat Tops
Mountains has remained largely untouched because of its remote
location on the White River Plateau between the Colorado and the
White Rivers.

Originally the domain of Ute Indians who fiercely defended their
"Shining Mountains," this land was set aside by President Benjamin
Harrison in 1891 as the second oldest forest reserve in the nation,
after Yellowstone. The forest floor rises abruptly from irrigated river
valleys into steep canyons rimmed by dark stands of Colorado blue
spruce, Douglas fir, and ponderosa pine. Higher still are magnificent
aspen groves. Though perhaps three-fourths of the main Ute Trail
corridor has been discovered, its exact location will always remain
a mystery, and there are many research riddles that will never be
solved. Some sacred sites close to the trail have been identified;
others will probably remain unknown and hopefully undisturbed.
Few other Indian trails in the central Rocky Mountains are in such
pristine condition and present such an opportunity for a partnership
in preservation involving the three Ute tribes, the USFS, the BLM,
and private landowners.

Understanding the trail and the migratory patterns of the Ute Indians requires stepping back in time half a millennium. The Ute, who traveled in family bands with older relatives and small children, followed the landscape and terrain contours in a way that four-wheel-drive vehicles cannot. Walking the trail today represents a unique wilderness experience because the trail widens to almost three miles and then funnels down to narrow thirty-yard passageways between ecotones, where open meadows and small aspen groves give way to thick, dark spruce. Unlike many trails within federally designated National Wilderness areas, the Ute Trail is not an overused, deeply rutted bridle path.

The trail corridor is of sufficient width and length to evoke a sense of prehistoric and historic travel, and it offers a unique passport back in time. A key component of finding and identifying the Ute Trail is to think about Indian usage of the forest, for it was excellent summer range for small bands of Ute families who came to the Flat Tops from the south, moving up the Roaring Fork River Valley and from Utah to the west from the Uintah and Piceance Creek basins. These close-knit family bands came to hunt, fish, gather berries and seeds, collect eagle feathers, and worship among the tall stands of Engelmann spruce and high mountain meadows. Ute use of the forest was part of an age-old rhythmic cycle that began about the middle of May and ended around the first of November or when early snows began to close off the high country. The Ute used the lush mountain meadows in the summer and then descended in the winter from 10,000 feet to the warmer basin and plateau country, some 5,000 feet in elevation.

The Ute lived off the land and knew the landscape intimately. They also kept a wary eye out for Shoshone, Arapaho, Cheyenne, and even Sioux warriors who may have ventured into the Ute's high mountain domain from Wyoming and the northeast in search of food or the spoils of war (including women and children to take as hostages). Consequently, the Ute Trail usually commands a high lookout and follows the ridgelines rather than adhering to the course of streambeds.

The trail is still intact because of the historic remoteness of western Colorado and the Ute's successful attempts to deter Anglo settlement and live in peace with whites until 1879. Under the skilled leadership of Chief Ouray, who was fluent in Ute, Spanish, and English, and because of the belligerence of Chief Colorow, the Ute managed to keep white settlement out of western Colorado through a series of treaties and through friendships with whites, among them the Spanish friars Dominguez and Escalante, Kit Carson, John Wesley Powell, and a host of Colorado citizens. As late as the 1870s, Colorado remained a frontier and the carefully negotiated Treaty of 1868 provided the Ute with over sixteen million acres on Colorado's Western Slope. Considering that throughout history, the Ute probably never numbered more than 4,000 to 5,000, their defense of their mountain homeland against other Indian tribes and white incursions is remarkable.

When prospectors discovered gold in Colorado in 1858, hordes of miners poured into Ute territory, so the federal government requested a treaty designating reservation boundaries. In the Treaty of 1868, the Ute received title to one-third of Colorado territory, and they had the right to bar any whites from entering the Western Slope and the peaks they called "The Shining Mountains." Though Ouray had negotiated a generous treaty and though he was at the height of his diplomatic powers, he told reporters, "Agreements the Indian makes with the government are like the agreement a buffalo makes with the hunter after it has been pierced by many arrows. All it can do is lie down and give in." Ouray insisted that the treaty be made "final forever."

But white settlers continued to encroach on Ute lands, and prospectors discovered gold in the rugged San Juan Mountains of southwest Colorado. Six years after the treaty guaranteeing the Ute one-third of Colorado, Chief Ouray and others signed the Brunot Treaty of 1873, in which the Ute agreed to give up the mineral-rich San Juans. In that year, teams of geographers and geologists working with F. V. Hayden began to map the territory of Colorado from their base at the White River Agency. It was the network of Ute Indian trails that provided access for the first organized expedition of American scientists into the Colorado Rockies. The white men's survey instruments would ultimately endanger Indian landownership, though the Ute could not conceive of dividing the mountains by lines of latitude and longitude.

The surveys would continue for three seasons and would represent some of the most remarkable work ever done in the United States, with sextant and transit triangulating straight survey lines off the highest peaks and drawing in canyons, creeks, and alluvial fans in remarkable scale and detail. The report of the Hayden Survey was published in Washington in 1877. In the following May, Nathan C. Meeker became the Indian agent at the White River Agency, and in a gesture of friend ship, Chief Douglas guided Meeker to Trapper's Lake and up to Marvine Lake on the Flat Tops in June.

Five years after the first surveyors climbed onto the Flat Tops, prospectors discovered silver at Leadville, Colorado. In that same year, three miners traveled down the Eagle River to the point where it joined the Colorado River, and they crossed the river onto the Ute Reservation. After hundreds of years of quiet use by prehistoric and historic Indian families and small bands, the eastern edge of the Ute Trail was about to be extensively used by prospectors in a burst of activity. While miners and prospectors swarmed up the trail in the spring of 1879, conditions at the White River Agency continued to deteriorate as sanctimonious Nathan Meeker insisted that the horse-loving Ute give up their nomadic ways for farming. But the Ute detested the plow.

Meeker became increasingly agitated with the Ute, who wanted him replaced. After being harassed and shoved by Chief Jack, Meeker sent a desperate message for U.S. troops to ride south from the railhead at Rawlins, Wyoming. On September 25, 1879, soldiers camped on Fortifi cation Creek, and four days later, the Milk Creek Siege began. Desperate Ute killed Agent Meeker and ten others because once the soldiers had crossed onto the reservation, the Indians considered the armed trespass an act of war.

Chief Ouray had tried to defuse the Meeker situation, but whites in Denver would have nothing but the complete removal of the Ute. In other words, an entire nation would be forced off their ancestral lands because of the depredations of a few. By 1880, a hastily written treaty in Washington, D.C., forced the White River Ute out of western Colorado and onto the Uintah Indian Reservation in northeast Utah. On September 4, 1881, Ute Reservation lands in western Colorado were thrown open to settlement and official entry by the General Land Office.

As soon as the Ute were forced to leave their beloved homeland, cattlemen rushed in from Texas and New Mexico and ran huge herds of bony longhorn and Hereford cattle on the public domain. Tempers flared between cowboys and settlers as immigrant families began to homestead the creek and river bottoms, but it was nothing like the antipathy be tween the cattlemen and sheepmen as vast sheep herds moved east from the Great Basin. On the high Book Cliffs above the Colorado River Valley, masked and armed cowboys routinely lassoed sheepherders, tied them to their sheep wagons, and beat them severely, then the cowboys would whoop and holler and drive the herds off the steep cliffs to their deaths in the shaley bottoms. Mormon sheepmen and Mexican and Greek immigrant herders knew that safety and valuable grass could be found in the high mountain meadows of the White River Plateau, but how could they get there without arousing the wrath of the cattlemen? How could a few herders move thousands of sheep almost sixty miles and not be seen?

The answer to the prejudice of the day and the reason the Old Ute Indian Trail can now be located a century after the Ute were banished was that on the west side of the White River National Forest, the herders found the historic Indian trail and quickly and quietly adopted it. As they moved sheep eastward up and out of the Piceance Basin, in their own way, four generations of sheepmen and thousands of bleating sheep have performed a unique service; they have protected a valuable cultural resource by following one of the basic precepts of historic preservation— continued traditional use.

Existing archaeological features include what could be the only known high-altitude mountain bison hunting blind of piled stones, from which aboriginal hunters stalked herds of a buffalo species now extinct. Over the decades, mountain bison skulls have been found on the Flat Tops, but this was the first time a hunting blind was identified from which prehistoric hunters would have prepared to hunt with spears and, later, bows. Near a high-altitude lake, the team also identified distinct patterns in the rock where stones had been moved to either side of the trail to permit easier travel with horse-pulled travois. As Ernest Ingersoll explained in his 1883 book *Knocking Round the Rockies,* "A trail is not a road; it is not even a path sometimes. As the word indicates, it is the mark left on the ground by something dragged, as lodge-poles, which the Indians fasten to the saddles of horses." But perhaps the most interesting find on the Flat Tops, in addition to rock arrangements for sacred vision quest sites, was a series of lichen-covered stone cairns as tall as a man. Four of these cairns stand as silent sentinels on a windswept plain at an elevation of 10,000 feet. They possibly mark an intersection of trails, and though within the last hundred years sheepherders have also piled up stone cairns in different parts of the forest and added stones to older archaeological features, these cairns seem ancient.

The exact location of the Ute Trail on the Flat Tops in Colorado is not public information because U.S. Forest Service managers and the Ute Trail Research Team are preparing a draft management plan whose primary objective is to prevent degradation of the existing resource. Baseline monitoring of remote cultural sites is essential, as is extensive consultation with the three Ute Tribes—the Northern Ute, Southern Ute, and Ute Mountain Ute—to discern what amount of management participation the tribes want. As archaeologist Mike Metcalf noted, "The Utes appear to see the trail as part of a larger context which includes access to sacred sites and protection of them." He also explained that "the trail itself has less meaning than the landscape and Ute spirituality connected with traditional homelands."

On dozens of national forests, pioneer packers, bushwhackers, and settlers carved trails through the woods out of a desire to cover distance between two points. But Indians traveled differently, and to hike or ride the Ute Trail is to experience the forest through the eyes of its first inhabitants. Much remains to be done, especially with respect to Ute Indian sacred sites and the cultural values those sites represent. The National Register process has not been completed, but just as the Ute preserved and protected the Flat Tops for centuries prior to the white man's arrival, so they should now be a part of the Ute Trail planning and management process. The potential is exciting: to keep intact for generations what may be the longest high-altitude Indian trail left in the United States.

Spring Ritual

Audrey DeLella Benedict
from *Valley of the Dunes:*
Great Sand Dunes National Park
and Preserve

Naturalist Audrey DeLella Benedict and photographers Bob
Rozinski and Wendy Shattil celebrate Colorado's San Luis Valley.
Here, Benedict describes the migratory visits of the sandhill cranes,
the "oldest modern bird species on earth."

With the coming of spring, the San Luis Valley's wetlands welcome tens of thousands of northbound avian travelers—sandhill cranes, herons, white-faced ibis, geese, ducks, grebes, shorebirds, and songbirds of every stripe. The skies are alive with continual arrivals and departures, endless lifting and settling of ducks, and the splendid cacophony of a thousand different voices.

My own spring ritual—with binoculars in hand—always involves a March migration to Monte Vista National Wildlife Refuge to mark winter's end with a spirit-lifting infusion of sandhill crane music. The refuge, which hosts nearly 20,000 migrating sandhill cranes and has the highest nesting densities of ducks in North America, combines a network of irrigated wetlands and fields planted solely to support resident breeders as well as migrants. For several weeks each spring and fall, the San Luis Valley serves as a staging ground and "refueling" stop for the cranes along a migratory pathway that may be millions of years old.

The crane family *(Gruidae)* is one of the oldest bird families in the world, having made its first appearance roughly 65 million years ago. Fossil wing bones of sandhill cranes *(Grus Canadensis)* exactly identical to those we see today have been found in Wyoming and Nebraska and are thought to be at least 9 million years old—making the sandhill crane the oldest modern bird species on earth.

We know that prehistoric people hunted sandhill cranes in the San Luis Valley for thousands of years and that the Spanish explorers referred to the nearby San Juan Mountains as *las sierras de las grullas* or "mountains of the cranes." In a rock shelter above Limekiln Creek, along the southwestern edge of the valley, the image of a large flying bird—undoubtedly a sandhill crane—has been pecked into the smoke-blackened wall of the shelter. Though the age of this rock art panel is unknown, the small geometric design below the bird is thought to be a Puebloan crane clan symbol. Sandhill cranes were held in such high regard by Puebloan peoples up and down the Rio Grande that lessons drawn from the crane's lifeway and habits are found in traditional "teaching" stories told to children. Cranes also play a signal role in secret rituals practiced by the Tewas, the Zuni, and the Hopi.

Though the sandhill cranes are still a long way off, I can hear the first armada calling on the wing long before I actually see them—a formidable, dignified procession across the dusk-stilled sky. Soon, a single, trumpet like horn note reverberates from overhead and the cranes begin swirling down like parachutists to land in the field directly before me. In the distance I can see and hear hundreds more in the fading light, long wavering lines of cranes coming from every direction to spend the night within the safety of their legions. The sandhill cranes will spend several weeks alternating flights to traditional sites each evening for roosting and to farm fields and meadows each dawn to forage and build fat reserves for the final flight to the nesting grounds. There is much chattering between them as the cranes settle in for the night, the din diminishing as sleep comes to the flock, heads gracefully tucked under their wings. As the moon rises and cold settles like a blanket over the fields, I see thousands of crane shapes illuminated in silvered moonlight, and I leave them to their well deserved rest.

Writing in "Marshland Elegy," Aldo Leopold described the voice of the sandhill crane as "the trumpet in the orchestra of evolution." His eloquent words speak not only to the antiquity of cranes but also to an anatomical adaptation that lies at the heart of the crane's remarkable voice. Birds produce sounds at the base of the trachea (windpipe), not at the top, as mammals do. In general, bigger birds have longer tracheas and a deeper timbre to their voices—especially among those species whose calls must travel across vast distances. The sandhill crane's long trachea, acting much like a French horn, serves to increase the harmonic range of the vocalizations and improve acoustical transmission. The voices of calling cranes embody the very spirit of wilderness—and a time when the whole world turned on seasonal rhythms.

The spring migratory stopover provides sandhill cranes with an opportunity to reestablish pair bonds and to engage in the elaborate courtship displays that have been celebrated in dance, prose, and legend in cultures throughout the world. Perhaps emboldened by the ancient energy of their rituals, sandhill cranes engage in animated "dance" maneuvers that include dipping, bowing, wing flapping, and leaps of twelve or more feet into the air. Dancing activity is most intense among the younger birds, subadults who have yet to breed. At times, a frenzy of dancing will spread contagiously through the flock, creating a spectacular and unforgettable show. As the urgency to move north to the breeding areas overcomes them, a few cranes at a time will launch themselves into the air with a great flapping of wings. Others follow until the whole sky seems filled with sandhill cranes—an aerial ballet, with birds climbing skyward on the spiraling thermals, their voices diminishing as they vanish amidst the mare's tails and blue sky on the northward journey.

Foreword

Laton McCartney
from *Across the Great Divide: Robert Stuart
and the Discovery of the Oregon Trail*

*In this introduction to Laton McCartney's book, the historic traces
of a legendary trail lead into the poignant story of one family's
journey—in this instance, the author's own.*

In June 1812, not quite six years after the return of Meriwether
Lewis and William Clark from the far reaches of the American
frontier, another expedition set out to cross the western half of
the continent.

Led by a young, Scottish-born fur trader and explorer, Robert Stuart, this seven-man party discovered a gateway through the Rocky
Mountains as well as much of the overland route across the western
half of the continent that would become the emigrant trail to Oregon
and California. This is an account of Stuart's remarkable journey
and the events that led up to it.

Today, Stuart's expedition has largely been forgotten, but it ranks
as one of the great adventure odysseys of nineteenth-century North
America. For me, it is an intensely personal narrative. Stuart was my
ancestor, a paternal grandfather four generations removed. I grew up
in the late 1940s and early 1950s on a remote ranch in southeastern
Wyoming, the son of a hard-drinking, Yale-educated cattleman from
Colorado and his New Haven-born wife. Set against the eastern slope
of the Medicine Bow Range, our ranch was traversed by an offshoot
of the century-old emigrant road Stuart had been the first to travel.

In the spring, when the wagon tracks were clearly visible in
the new grass, my sister and I used to follow the trail northwest
toward Elk Mountain in search of arrowheads as well as artifacts
discarded by the pioneers as their wagon trains struggled to ascend
the foothills. Each year we'd discover new treasures—pieces of

crockery, cartridge casings, broken furniture, a cast-iron stove half submerged in the mud at the edge of Dutton Creek, even the badly weathered torso of a wooden doll.

The trail and its history loomed large in my imagination. Lying awake with the relentless Wyoming wind whistling outside our ranch house, I read about the Grattan Massacre, a dispute over an emigrant's stray cow that triggered twenty-five years of warfare with the Sioux; the ill-fated Donner expedition; and Marcus and Narcissa Whitman's pilgrimage to Oregon to salvage the souls of the Cayuses and Flatheads.

Owen Wister's *The Virginian* was set outside the town of Medicine Bow, just northeast of my family's ranch, and old Fort Laramie lay to the east on the far side of Laramie Peak. There, the young Francis Parkman made copious field notes for *The Oregon Trail,* and tens of thousands of emigrants rested and reconnoitered after coming up the Platte River Road, the first leg of their long westward journey.

Robert Stuart was the first nonnative American to travel the length of this road. A junior partner in one of John Jacob Astor's fur -trading ventures, he sailed to the mouth of the Columbia River in 1810. There, he and his shipmates established Astoria, the first American settlement on the Pacific Coast and the headquarters for what Astor hoped would develop into a frontier empire in the Northwest.

In June 1812, Stuart, then twenty-seven, was chosen to lead a small overland expedition back to St. Louis and New York. Two American-led expeditions had crossed the continent before him, that of Lewis and Clark in 1803–1806 and Wilson Price Hunt's, another of Astor's traders, in 1810–11. But Lewis and Clark's Corps of Discovery and Hunt had both journeyed up the Missouri and over the rugged, nearly impassable northern Rockies. Traveling from west to east for more than three thousand miles by canoe, on horseback, and ultimately by foot, Stuart and his six companions followed the mountains south until they came upon South Pass, the one gap in the three thousand-mile-long Rocky Mountain chain that was pass able by wagon. From there they continued east along the Sweetwater and Platte Rivers across present-day Wyoming and Nebraska. The path that this obscure young Scot and his eastbound companions blazed became the central route of America's expansion, the emigrant road that opened up the Far West to settlement.

A daguerreotype of Stuart and his wife, Betsy, hung in my grand-mother's house in Denver—venerated icons that embodied what my grandmother described as "the pioneer spirit." Stuart, the long-dead family patriarch, seemed a stern and foreboding figure whose dark, probing eyes seemed to scrutinize disapprovingly my tomboy sister, Dillon, and me whenever we came down from the ranch to visit.

As a boy I listened attentively to my grandmother's stories about Stuart's exploits, but I was far more partial to Indians, gunfighters, and cowboys than fur trader-explorers. Then, too, I associated Stuart with the Scottish side of the family and specifically my father, a difficult, domineering, sometimes violent man from whom I was estranged for much of my adult life. After being sent east to boarding school, I distanced myself from him—and my western roots—eventually settling in New York, a city my father loathed and feared in equal measure. It was only after my father finally gave up drinking in the mid-1970s that we reconciled and I began joining him on fishing trips out West.

It was on the last of those excursions, a weeklong trip to Wyoming in late July, that I first considered writing about Stuart and my western heritage. At the time, my father was suffering from throat cancer. Both of us knew he hadn't much time left.

We'd started our trip in Jackson Hole, fishing on a privately owned ranch just outside Teton Park, and then driven down to Pinedale, where we fished the Green and the New Fork rivers. Neither of us had much luck that last morning. We caught several middling rainbow trout and a few whitefish that my father would haul in impatiently and then discard, throwing them to the riverbank in disgust. Once whitefish got in a stream, he claimed, they proliferated and drove away the trout. He killed as many of them as he could.

Normally, we would have fished until the fading light made it impossible to see our flies on the river, but my father's dwindling energy reserves were spent, and a dark, malignant-looking thunder storm was working its way down the Wind River Range in our direction. With thunder sounding in the distance, we decided to head on back to town rather than wait for the rancher who was coming to pick us up at dusk and risk getting soaked.

Walking back to Pinedale, we suddenly came upon a Sublette County historical marker that was partially obscured by a stand of lodgepole pines. Although we'd been fishing in the area for several days, neither of us had noticed it before. "I'll be damned," my father said. "Look at this." He read the inscription aloud:

A Pause on the Journey

On Oct. 16, 1812, the Astorians Robert Stuart, Ramsay Crooks, Robert McClellan, Joseph Miller, Benjamin Jones, Francis LeClair and Andy Valle, traveling from Astoria to St. Louis, all their horses having been stolen by Indians, passed this way by foot and forded Pine Creek near here, the first whites known to have seen it. From Stuart's journal: "We forded another stream whose banks were adorned with many pines—near which we found an Indian encampment deserted about a month ago, with immense numbers of buffalo bones strewed everywhere; in center of camp a great lodge of pines and willows at west and three persons lay interred with feet to east; at head of each a large buffalo skull painted black; from lodge were suspended numerous ornaments and moccasins." Six days later on Oct. 22nd, they made the memorable discovery of the South Pass.

I had enough of the Irish mystic in me from my mother's side of the family to view our discovery as an epiphany, a sign from beyond the great veil. Here I was fishing with my dying father on a remote Wyoming outback, and we found that we'd been treading exactly the same path our ancestor had traversed nearly two centuries earlier. The dead greet the dying, appropriately at the site of what once had been an Indian burial lodge.

For an instant, I could envision Stuart and his men, gaunt and spectral, reconnoitering the deserted Indian lodge. My father, I'm sure, had a similar revelation. Certainly, he looked as if he had seen a ghost. "Imagine being the first white man to see this country," he said in a quiet voice.

We lingered at the marker for a few minutes, lost in our own thoughts, and then continued on into town, beating the rain by a matter of minutes.

Soon after, my father took his own life rather than endure further the cancer and the chemotherapy that left him racked with pain and nausea. In accordance with his wishes, my mother, sister, and I had him cremated in Denver, his hometown, and then drove up to an old friend's ranch in Wyoming to scatter his ashes over a favorite fishing hole on the North Platte.

Months later, in going through some of my father's possessions that had been in storage, I discovered the framed daguerreotype of the Stuarts that had hung in my by-then-deceased grandmother's living room in Denver.

There was also a privately published two-volume edition of Stuart family letters and a rare 1935 edition of *The Discovery of the Oregon Trail: Robert Stuart's Narratives of His Overland Trip Eastward from Astoria,* edited by the late western historian Philip A. Rollins. The latter includes the remarkable journal Stuart had kept during his ten- month-long trek across the continent. He'd written it using sap, berry juice, and even his own blood after he'd run out of ink. The original journal and traveling memoranda (the latter written after the expedition) had been used by Washington Irving without attribution as the basis for much of *Astoria,* his account of Astor's ill- fated trading venture. Years after Irving's death the journal was discovered tucked away in a cupboard in the author's Hudson River Valley house, Sunnyside.

Of Stuart's narrative, which eventually found its way into the William Robertson Coe Collection at the Beinecke Library at Yale University, Rollins wrote, "Compared with all the other overland diaries of the United States . . . Stuart's product seems to be out ranked only by the journals emanating from the Lewis and Clark expedition."

Stuart arrived in Oregon in 1811, returning in 1813. A few years later he went into business with Astor running the field operations of Astor's American Fur Company (AFC) from remote Mackinac Island in northern Michigan. I discovered copies of the AFC letters, including hundreds to and from Stuart, in various historical archives, including the New York Historical Society, only a few blocks from my home on Manhattan's Upper West Side.

Months later, in a conversation with a distant cousin, I learned that my grandmother's late sister in St. Paul had owned a collection of previously unpublished family letters including hundreds written by Robert and Betsy Stuart and their oldest daughter and her husband, Mary and Dr. George Franklin Turner, my forebears. Before she died, my great-aunt, an intensely private woman, indicated she wanted the letters destroyed because of their personal revelations. Happily, one of her daughters ignored her dictate and donated this vivid chronicle of frontier life to the Minnesota Historical Society.

Stuart's journals, the AFC records and correspondence, and the family letters lent Robert Stuart humanity and animation, revealing him as vulnerable and more appealing than I'd imagined. His journals make clear that Stuart, the seemingly intrepid, resolute voyager, had his moments of self-doubt, trepidation, and wrongheadedness. He was, after all, an entrepreneur, not an explorer. He'd come to the Pacific Northwest simply to make his fortune in the fur trade, yet during his stay in the wilderness, he emerged as a pioneer western naturalist of the first rank, a perceptive student of Native American cultures, and one of America's most important, if least known, explorers.

The earlier Lewis and Clark expedition had turned the nation's eyes to the vast wilderness west of the Mississippi, but it was really Robert Stuart who opened the door to westward expansion.

5 ✣ Looking for More

Sometimes we want to know and experience more than can be seen on the world's surfaces, even when those surfaces are rich, intricate, and challenging. We wonder what important stories of geology, evolution, history, ecology, and spirit lie hidden beyond or beneath our ordinary surroundings and daily lives. We search for these stories in the understandings and intuitions of cultures that have lived for many centuries in the West, in books driven by new questions and rich new knowledge, in our own curiosities and imaginations. With each piece in this section, we embark on such a search.

The Voice of the Crane

SueEllen Campbell
from *Even Mountains Vanish: Searching for Solice in an Age of Extinction*

This selection describes a winter afternoon in northern New Mexico, where peace and warfare intersect in troubling ways. The questions that arise here trigger SueEllen Campbell's exploration of the complexities of place and the intimate relationships between catastrophe and creation, despair and hope.

We had driven in earlier that afternoon across the Pajarito Plateau, past the bold signs for Los Alamos and into Bandelier National Monument, where we'd stopped at the rim of Frijoles Canyon to have our sandwiches in the sun. We'd been talking about our last visit a few winters before, when we had hiked down a deserted hanging trail to the Rio Grande. To our surprise, the river was frozen, and we sat alone on the rocky bank admiring the complicated textures of the ice, its turquoise gleams and shadows. Steller's jays flew about calling brightly, their cobalt feathers brilliant in the slanted light, and the ice creaked and sighed. Calm air and water, the world asleep under winter's white weight: in that tranquil and lovely place, it seemed, we could rest ourselves in a moment out of time. We'd remembered that serenity, and now, on this warm day in February, we had returned hoping for more.

So when we'd finished our lunch and my husband had wandered off to explore, I found a smooth spot on the ground, rolled my jacket into a pillow, and stretched out on my back. The air felt cool and clean, the sun warm against my skin, my every breath was fragrant with piñon and juniper, and a pair of jays above me flashed like blue coal against the sky. I lay still, tried to stop the clatter of voices in my head, and waited for that infrequent but familiar feeling that some space inside me was opening up, making room for a kind of peace.

Usually I could bring on this transformation without much trouble, given a little time to myself in a quiet place outdoors, especially where the natural world seemed healthy. Even here, where the protected ruins and wilderness lands of the national monument lie immediately next to Los Alamos National Laboratory, I'd always been able to close my mind to things I didn't want to think about, put aside distress and let beauty in. Driving by the laboratory, I'd think for a few uneasy minutes about the irony of its location, how the top-secret home of the first nuclear bomb had been hidden so close above this placid canyon with its long-abandoned cliff houses and kivas. I'd offer a kind of ritual grimace, and then, the way I might shake loose from the sight of a highway crash, I'd turn my thoughts to the simpler scenes ahead.

Not today, though. Since my last visit here, the fifty-year anniversary of Hiroshima had passed. I'd been reading about the history of nuclear bombs and about radioactive contamination in the West. And I'd been typing my father's autobiography, learning about the time he spent during World War II as a cryptographer in the Pacific. I knew just enough more now to feel confused, just enough that I couldn't clear my mind.

So I lay brooding about aggression and fear, territoriality and defensiveness, creation and catastrophe. I thought about how the ancestral Puebloan people we often call the Anasazi had built their lives all across this part of the continent, stayed for centuries, then moved on for reasons we'll never know for certain, maybe pushed out by drought, by internal warfare, by violent invaders, how the people of this canyon and plateau might simply have moved nearby to today's Cochiti and San Ildefonso Pueblos, as their inhabitants believe. These small houses carved into high, inaccessible cliffs, then left empty for time and weather: what terrors might they have sheltered, what protections offered and lost?

I wondered about what might be buried in the volcanic soil under my back. Obsidian lance points ten thousand years old, relics of killings long forgotten? The traces of my own culture's weapons, lost bits of plutonium or uranium, hot pools or messy dumps of radioactive wastes, stray poisonous particles moving invisibly from earth to grass to deer? I imagined my father on Iwo Jima, a kid from Kansas swimming in the ocean around that wrecked island, encrypting and decrypting messages about the movements ofb-29bombers, while on this sunny plateau in northern New Mexico, scientists devised the bombs that would send him home to meet and marry my mother.

Was this just the same old sad story, the one about human violence, the endless damage we do, may always have done, to ourselves, each other, everything around us? Yes, I thought, but that didn't make it simple. I couldn't even tell myself that if humans are violent and destructive, the natural world, at least, is peaceful and enduring, not while I lay with my back pressed tightly against the remnants of enormous volcanic explosions and the cold winter earth stole my own body's warmth.

The longer I thought, the more confused I became. With every loop and tangle, the ironies grew more complex and elusive, the resonances more unsettling.

And yet this afternoon was too lovely for such dark broodings, the sky too blue for a heavy heart, and a pair of golden eagles had appeared above me, floating in big, easy circles, tugging me back into the sunny present. I pulled my small binoculars from their case and fiddled with the focus until I could see the shapes of the eagles' heads.

"What's that sound?" John asked, suddenly back beside me.

"Cranes!"

"No, it's still winter. It can't be."

But it was, that unmistakable gargle of sandhill cranes flying high overhead, higher than the eagles, moving north along the Rio Grande for their age-old spring stopover in the marshes of southern Colorado.

The sun poured through their long, narrow wings, first the warm color of ripe wheat, then a flash of white or charcoal as they angled and curved. They moved in a long, wavering V, until a score or so would break loose, arc sideways, and spiral back, brightening and darkening against the steady light.

Later in the afternoon we walked along the trail at the bottom of Frijoles Canyon. The air was chilly in the shade of the ponderosa pines, and we stepped carefully, for the patches of ice were doubly slick with the day's melting. The great wall to the north glowed like soft gold, and high above the mirroring creek, the crumbling front walls of ancient houses echoed the curves and angles of erosion. I stopped to read each interpretive sign. One explained how the houses had been carved with the sharp edges of basalt into the softer tuff of the cliffs and plateau. What a lovely idea, I thought, to make a home in a volcano with tools from a volcano. I leaned forward into the flaky cinnamon-colored plates of bark on a ponderosa, pressed my nose into one of the deeper crevices, and breathed in its warm vanilla scent.

A squirrel chattered up ahead, and I heard the short chip of a chickadee as I read another sign. We were standing in an ecotone, it said, a transition zone, where members of different biological communities mingle. I looked around. Narrow-leaf cottonwoods along the creek; the odd little horsetails that in summer would flourish along the damp banks like miniature groves of green bamboo; tall ponderosas here on the canyon's shady side, where the snow stays longest; curly-leafed Gambel oak with its bitter, nourishing acorns. A few other tourists passed by, one group speaking with British accents, another in German, a third in something that sounded to me like Russian.

I felt bombarded by messages. Everything around me was telling me something important, it seemed, but what?

I studied the pine needles strewn on the trail. Some were frozen into the ice, but others were loose, and I picked one up to feel its textures, its three long needles bound by a dark knot at one end. It was still flexible, and I began to braid its strands together as I walked. Piles of scat, greenish gray and full of white fur, announced the presence of coyotes, and the cutoff brushy ends of pine branches lay scattered at random, a sign of squirrels feeding on the trees' inner bark. A raven glided along the cliff top without once moving its wings.

Then another filament of cranes slid across the narrow slice of sky. Their strange music opened up the silence, that ancient and enigmatic gargling, and listening to them in the still winter day, I saw for an instant how much was happening here.

Above me birds were floating on thermals and migrating along invisible paths. The fallen cones of the ponderosas were expanding and popping, their seeds preparing to send out tendrils, and the leaves of oaks and cottonwoods were darkening into soil. Coyotes, foxes, mountain lions, all were sleeping somewhere not far away. Above me on the plateau, hidden caches of radioactive elements were throwing out their particles and rays. The cliffs I looked at, the crumbling yellow cups of houses, and the ground beneath my feet were eroding under water and ice, the mountains were melting, even the plate holding the continent was edging south and west, and the planet was spinning through space at an ungraspable speed— all as I meandered along the trail, in and out of the chilly shade, thinking my human thoughts.

Maybe this was all about time, all this afternoon's cryptic messages, my murmuring uneasiness, about how long things last, and in what forms. I knew so little of the history of this place—that Los Alamos National Laboratory had been here half a century, the cliff houses seven or eight centuries, humans a hundred centuries. The cranes had come earlier, certainly, but how much? Before these mountains, maybe even before the continents and oceans had taken their familiar places? I'd read on another sign that all this earth had emerged from the Jemez volcano in two great waves of eruptions, 1.1 and 1.4 million years ago. I knew this wasn't long in geological or evolutionary terms, but such numbers meant nothing real to me. I had no sense of their scale, no context for even beginning to understand them. And the other creatures around me, the ponderosas and horsetails, the fat dark Abert's squirrel that just now ran up the trail and stopped not four feet in front of us, with its huge tail, long black ear tufts, and an expression, it seemed, of hope—how old were these species? For how many centuries had they lived here, in this place?

Maybe I could learn the answers to some of these questions. Then maybe I could begin to understand this scene, this after noon in this place, hold its actors together in my mind in some proper proportion—the present and many pasts, sudden cataclysms and the peace of winter waters, atomic bombs and sand hill cranes.

The needles I'd been braiding together in my hands sprang apart.

Trail Notes—
Four Corners—1986

Peter Anderson
from *First Church of the Higher Elevations:
Mountains, Prayer, and Presence*

*Peter Anderson celebrates the healing powers of both snowy
mountain peaks and "inward" summits. In this selection, he
describes how the "heat, prayer, and fellowship" of sweatlodge
ceremonies help deepen his spiritual life.*

I left the Arkansas Valley in 1985 and ended up living for a while
in Durango, a lively mountain town in southwestern Colorado.
There, as a stringer for the *Denver Post,* I wrote feature stories.
Periodically, I would pitch story ideas to the state desk and more
often than not they were interested. So I was able to range freely
around southwestern Colorado and occasionally into Utah, writing
the kind of features I enjoyed—relieved to have left that part of my
old beat that included school board and town council meetings. One
story idea led me out to Alan Neskahi's powwow south of Cortez and
into an experience of prayer that would nudge me further along on
the trail of the Spirit.

In addition to putting on an annual powwow, Alan had dedicated
his home—also known as the Spirit-Life Center—to a ministry that
melded Navajo tradition with the teachings of Christianity. Like his
father before him, Alan was a circuit-riding evangelist of sorts, min-
istering to make shift gatherings on the "rez." Back in the summer of
1986, I arrived at his door, thinking that he would be a great profile
story. With reporter's pad and camera close at hand, I sat down on the
couch in his living room. Alan settled his burly frame into a wellworn
easy chair. Grandchildren played at his feet. His wife and daughter
spoke quietly over coffee at the kitchen table. He wasn't a man to be

rushed into anything, nor was he inclined toward formality of any kind. He was more interested in talking about an upcoming powwow than he was in talking about himself.

"You oughta come out to the powwow this weekend," he said. I muttered something about not wanting to intrude.

"All people have their place . . . just like the four directions and the four colors," he said. "We come together to share out here. You oughta come out . . . maybe you'll find something."

That weekend, I drove out south of Cortez, less interested in writing a story and more interested in just being present. I arrived at Neskahi's well before the sun had come up over the La Platas, in order to join an early morning "sweat" that began each day of the powwow. Even though I had no reason to feel anything but welcome out at the Neskahis'—I knew that Alan's invitation had been sincere—I felt a little self-conscious as I walked out through the still empty cottonwood arbor that surrounded the dancing area, worried, I suppose, that I would land myself in a crowd of gawking white spectators, or worse, starry-eyed Indian wanna-bes.

Right around daybreak, I met a couple of Alan's sons who came home every year to help out with the powwow.

Out by the bent-willow sweat lodge that stood beyond the arbor, beyond the arroyo, beyond the tall clumps of sage, and beside a cool stream of water that ran through an irrigation ditch, they were lighting a fire with a rolled up newspaper. "If this were a real traditional sweat," Arly said, "we'd be lighting this with the *Navajo Times*."

"Building this fire is like a guy tying his own noose," said Chuck, an Anglo friend who had become something of a regular out at the Neskahis'. Meanwhile Art Neskahi pitch-forked hunks of lava-rock into the flames. It wasn't until the rocks had been taken into the sweat lodge and a canvas flap had sealed us in darkness that I began to feel that noose.

Eight of us sat in a circle around those rocks.

Art splashed them with a ladle of water that hissed into steam. My lungs ached. I bent over to shield my face, gasping for air until I had the common sense to hunker down, face forward into my lap as close as I could get to the dirt floor where the heat was less intense. I tried to mop the sweat off of my forehead with a bundled clump of sage before it poured down into my eyes. Then came more water and another wave of hissing steam. In that dark heat, even a long-delinquent Episcopalian like myself could find reason to pray.

As with any sweat lodge, this canvas-covered dome had been intended as a place for prayer. It took me a while to realize how the heat had focused my attention in such a visceral way, on each breath, on each drink of water, on each song, on each prayer. In that dark heat, I heard songs whose notes would have flown off the scales in any hymnal. And I heard words spoken that could have come right out of the *Book of Common Prayer*.

Art later told me that the sweat lodge was a place where he had been able to honor his own Navajo tradition along with the teachings of Christianity. In the darkness that day, his prayers had indeed embodied the spirit as well as the language of both traditions.

For a day or two afterwards, I would notice the faint smell of the sage that had been baked into my pores. And that would remind me of dirt and sweat, of rock and water, of dark and light, of one breath and then another . . . sacraments that had grounded me. And like the sage, the essence of the prayers and songs we shared would linger somehow long after I had gone home to Durango, along with a vague reassurance that something like the Holy Spirit was alive and well.

I kept going back to Neskahi's. Once a month, we'd catch word that Art was going to run a sweat. About a half dozen people, Navajos and Anglos, would gather out by the fire. Taking swigs of water out of plastic jugs, we watched the flames and made light of the fact that we would soon be basting in the dark. Some months later, a few days before I left to begin a graduate program at the University of Wyoming, I joined the other "sweathogs," as we had come to call ourselves, for one last experience of heat, prayer, and fellowship.

"When the wind whips through Laramie," said one of my friends afterwards, "think of us down here sweating in the dark." I did think of them. Often. Never before had I experienced a form of shared worship with that much spiritual voltage. Nor had I sensed the kind of vulnerability that I heard expressed in that dark heat.

As it turned out, Art eventually grew weary of running the sweat. He began to find more sustenance in the Native American Church. No one else could sustain that curious blend of traditions that had offered a kind of temporary shelter for a few wayfaring souls.

A few years later, I would follow the lead of an old sweat lodge friend into the prayerful silence of Quaker meeting. But it was in that dark heat out at Neskahi's that an inter est in prayer began to grow in me. And it was in that dark heat where I began to understand prayer as a way into the center, the inward summit—that "little plot," as Dante put it, "for which we wax so fierce."

Snake Calendar

Craig Childs
from *Soul of Nowhere:*
Traversing Grace in a Rugged Land

Craig Childs' essay collection is a physical and metaphysical exploration of the deserts to the west and south of the Rockies, including parts of the route of the Colorado River. In this story of a winter solstice visit to a petroglyph in Utah, he contemplates the way that these arid canyons are a "massive calendar, a place bound to the sky."

I left in the morning long before the sun. Stars bathed my movements. Devin was still in his bag. He would catch up later. I walked west, aiming toward the red-eyed star of Orion. It began setting over the far cliffs as I dropped through the first leading canyons.

The land came visible under a thin, watery light. I could barely see fins rising ahead of me, sequential outlines that were the secret to knowing how to navigate this place. I walked a memory of benches and small back tracks from years of travel to the snake, a cut between walls that dropped one after the next, a huge staircase leading through a notch into a basin. A falling star streaked into the southern sky, breaking into a shower of pieces before dissolving, flushing into a green line, never allowed to touch ground. The eastern sky held the final cut of a crescent moon, almost a new moon. In every object around me, in the sky and on the earth, I saw this calendar. The universe seemed poised, each item in perfect place.

The moon was the most glaring of these items for the moment. Clear as a Cheshire grin, it hovered low in the sky, sickle thin. Everyday and night the moon rises in a different place at a different time, then every month it is somewhere else again. Among the idyllic cycles of the sun and seasons, the moon is an alluring nemesis. It crosses at unorthodox angles, swinging drunkenly over the horizons.

Fancifully, I thought of the nearby snake as a solar and lunar balance. It has the sun's bearing, but with the moon's data. The length of its body bears six troughs and seven crests, adding up to thirteen, the number of new moons in the year. Within the confines of a solar year, the moon gets abridged, allowed to complete only twelve and a half of its own cycles, which causes a disparity between moon time and sun time. At the snake, lunar phases could be counted starting at the summer solstice arrowhead. Working down the snake's body, every trough and crest would be marked by each month of the moon. The last moon of the lunar cycle would land in the final trough of the snake's tail, exactly one solar year after the moon-counting began, the moment that the next arrowhead of sunlight touches the head of the snake, the moment to begin counting again. Calendars for the moon and the sun would balance out across this snake.

As I walked, twilight met the moon above the horizon and began washing it away. I dropped from view of both Orion and the fading moon, winding toward a broad opening between fins. Crossing this clearing, I heard a raven coming through, its wings flapping hard against the cold. I stopped to watch it pass. Up the other side, I scrambled through house-sized boulders that formed a steep three-hundred foot apron below a cliff. As I came to the foot of the cliff I saw the snake within arm's reach of the ground. I stopped there, letting my heart slow from the climb. My eyes moved across the entire plane of the cliff, and I could not bring them back to the snake for at least another minute, taking in the angles of rock and the distances around me.

The snake is always a startling find, even knowing it is here, like coming across a Picasso painting lying on its side in an alley. It is literally in the middle of nowhere, boulders unfolded randomly beneath it. The horizontal body carries a sensuous tension flexing thirty feet from head to tail. It had been chiseled into the flesh of deep red sandstone, revealing the much paler rock within. When I came closer I stopped again and lifted my gloved hand in the air, tracing its ophidian crests and troughs. Curves spent themselves across the wall like water.

If you sat in the desert for a year with a clock and a Gregorian calendar, you would find that your time does not match what you see in the world around you. The snake, the stars, the sun, and the moon belong to an interlocking design. We fool ourselves with our inventions. The gears of true time are not round like those of the clock. The earth travels at different speeds during different times of the year, slinging faster and slower around the sun, making European winters eight days shorter than those in Australia. Lunar and solar cycles set up a complex rhythm obeying doublets and triplets, not the singular boxes of weekdays and months. We are made to look like simpletons the way we spoon-feed ourselves with our artless time of minutes, hours, and days, leap years thrown in to jury-rig our twelve months so that they don't fall into disrepair. We add and subtract sixty minutes of daylight saving time to our seasons to make our workdays more efficient, our heads buried in business while around us these flawless patterns pass like the hand of God.

I kept still in the cold, waiting in this place where true time shows itself. Soon the sun arrived. Light soaked each high point of stone hundreds of feet above. Shadows slid back into their crevices. Breezes came up as the cold sink of morning lazily rolled over itself. When the sun touched the head of the snake, it was nothing like summer solstice. Summer light had been pure white. This was the molten color of red curry. Instead of a discrete arrowhead, now came a two-hundred-foot wave of light. Absolutely vertical, it spanned the height of the cliff like an opening theater curtain.

Every tie that I had to the night sky came to me. This was the convergence of unimaginably expansive spheres—the inviolable sky, and the forged land. The snake had been slipped into place, a knot binding the two. I stood at the meeting point as these forces silently crossed each other like galaxies sliding together, and then apart.

When the sun finally moved beyond the snake's tail, warming the rock face until I felt it on my skin, I heard a peculiar, metallic sound. It twanged musically far in the distance, barely audible. I turned from the snake and looked out. The thing, whatever it was, plucked rhythmically. Perplexed, I traced the sound to a high notch I had come through earlier. There, Devin sat against a boulder playing a Jew's harp, snapping the metal tong against his open mouth. He was at my eye level a mile away. How long had he been there? Had he watched the light come across the snake?

I found a place to sit in the boulders, resting in the warmth of my clothes and the new sun. I listened to Devin's performance. With all of this fantastic consequence swirling around me, holy alignments striking down everywhere, Devin was a strange Puck in the rocks. Humans, I thought, what fantastic creatures we are, spinning like dervishes in these forever domains of star paths and canyons, grasping the extent of this landscape in one moment, forgetting in another. We lay out maps for ourselves as if we cannot see clearly enough with our own eyes. At the same time we expand beyond the farthest edges of our girded maps. We are perfect for this place. Never still and never simple.

Solace of Dinosaur Ridge

Richard F. Fleck
from *Breaking through the Clouds*

*Richard Fleck describes his lifetime among great peaks, from
Colorado's San Juan Mountains to Japan's Mount Fuji. Here, he
finds both an opportunity for quiet reflection and an imaginative
means of time travel—all on a ridgeline just twenty minutes from
downtown Denver.*

> *Quick iguanadons*
> *Pitter pat along muddy*
> *Beach with bright green eyes*

Dinosaur Ridge has be come an essential and necessary ingredi-
ent in my life since our move to Denver from a small university
town on the wild and open prairies of Wyoming. Where would
I have the freedom to roam and think in the urban sprawl of Denver?
Where could I botanize and examine fossils? How would I stand the
heat and smog of an August afternoon that would be cool and clear up
in Wyoming? Where could I quickly get away from people and sirens
and honking automobile horns? Piled on top of these concerns were
the pressures, after a few years, of my deanship in an inner-city college
with uniquely gifted yet disadvantaged students and a pressurized and
strained faculty struggling with ever- shrinking budgets.

Within weeks of our arrival from Laramie, I discovered the small
town of Morrison nestled behind an uplifted hogback formation called
Dakota Ridge or, more fondly, Dinosaur Ridge. This magical piece of
wild land lay only twenty-five minutes from central Denver. I took my
first stroll along the trail, following the ridge top well over 1,200 feet
above Denver after a heavy September frost. The city, smothered in
mist and cloud, completely disappeared. I breathed the ridge's fresh

and bracing air above the city's layers of cloud. That first walk along the ridge I repeated over and over again from September to April for twelve years straight. Sometimes I would go solo and sometimes with my wife and family, but most often with my little dog Mini, that golden English cocker spaniel with drooping ears and alert brown eyes.

This weekly ramble had become as much a ritual for me as my weekly walks on the Laramie plains. Summertime changed the Wyoming ritual with hikes in the alluring Snowy Range and now in the Front Range of Colorado. The high prairies of southern Wyoming have something very much in common with Dinosaur Ridge: namely, the Laramide Orogeny. Sixty to 75 million years ago, something within the Earth's core forced prehistoric swamplands (washed by the sea) upward. *If* four billion years could be transposed into one human life, the Laramide Orogeny raised the Rockies from sea level to almost three miles above sea level during the human equivalent time of two weeks.

The high, bald prairie of southern Wyoming rests at 7,200 feet, a thousand feet higher than the crests of Dinosaur Ridge. Inner forces of our planet are still pushing this land upward perhaps an eighth inch every century—not quite as fast as the growth rate of the Himalayas halfway around the globe. But the Laramie plains are essentially as flat as a seabed, while Dinosaur Ridge is a high, skinny ridge with downsloping Morrison Formation of gray beach rock on its east side and bright red Dakota Formation sandstone on its west side. The extreme north side is transected by Interstate 70. Why the name Dinosaur Ridge? Dinosaurs galore! Buried within the Dakota sandstones are the bones of stegosaurs, brontosaurs, and iguanodons, discovered by Arthur Lakes in 1877. Eventually, ten quarries yielded many fossils for rival museums in Philadelphia and New Haven. Today, Dinosaur Ridge is designated a national natural landmark. There are guided and self-guided tours along the base of both sides.

I love to visit one spot on the west side of Dinosaur Ridge that exposes the imprint of a brontosaurus made millions of years ago on an ancient muddy shoreline. The beast's immense weight sank him deep into the mud. His tracks probably filled in with algal ooze, helping to preserve the footprints in hardened mud-rock. Lower down the ridge are fossilized rib and skull bones of camarasaurs, carried by streams and deposited in deeper mud that has been hardened to sandstone and exposed by erosion to present-day viewers.

On the east side of Dinosaur Ridge lies a strangely rippled rock (formerly beach) that has been hardened to gray sandstone and tilted at a ludicrous angle of forty-five degrees. Within this beach are giant threetoed tracks of a vegetarian dinosaur known as the iguanodon. Alongside his prints are three-toed prehistoric bird prints of an ostrich like dinosaur. Early-morning shadows fill the tracks, clearly revealing their deep imprint. Because the beach is no longer sand but rock, and because the beach lies at an extreme angle, it is difficult to imagine a sea-level beach with heavy, humid air and swampy vegetation.

On one occasion, I took a quick walk along the east side of Dinosaur Ridge at sunset before boarding a jet the next morning bound for Charleston, South Carolina, to celebrate my brother's sixty-fifth birthday. Within hours of my arrival, I walked the Edisto Swamp Trail not far from the Georgia line with my brother and his children and their families. The geographic juxtaposition hit home. Here in the Edisto Swamp I breathed heavy, vaporous air, while hours earlier I breathed the bracing air of the high desert. At Edisto, I marveled at the delicate perfection of form and color of swamp orchids, the lush array of ferns and vine-covered southern pines, and the profusion of palmettos. On Dinosaur Ridge hours earlier, wind blew through the needles of pinyons and junipers. Deep in Edisto, I smelled mud and phosphates and thick vegetation. Up on Dinosaur, I smelled dust and rock and the scent of sage. Edisto provided a secure home for dinosaur like alligators and other reptiles like the cottonmouth water moccasin. Edisto became for me prehistoric, Precambrian Colorado, whose oozing muds would eventually harden and be uplifted to a multilayered Dinosaur Ridge.

Interstate 70cuts through Dinosaur Ridge and exposes all the layers of hardened pre-Laramide Orogeny sand and mud. As dinosaur like trucks and RVs revved their engines up i-70, Mini and I walked through a hundred million years of time. We stared up at the cut— through formations ranging in color from gray to black to red to brown and yellow. Even though the heavy traffic of i-70 roared like a troop of dinosaurs, we managed to journey backwards through time.

I let myself dream of what things looked like 300million years ago during the early Pennsylvanian Period, with its carboniferous jungles. I imagined looking westward to see an ancient mountain range 240 million years older than the present-day Rockies. This mountain range, like any other, had streams gushing off its slopes, depositing reddish quartz sand, silt grains, and clay. I tried to imagine these reddish deposits hardening into the red sandstone of the Fountain Formation and the Red Rocks Amphitheater of Beatles fame. But the only beetles I envisioned were black, creeping things on the muddy ooze of shorelines. What must it have been like 140 million years ago during the Jurassic Period? I imagined not seeing i-70 anymore and hearing the howl of meat-eating dinosaurs thumping through swamps and wetlands in an insufferably dank and humid atmosphere. What happened to Colorado? The only hint of its future existence lay in the gray and green and maroon clay-stone that would become the Morrison Formation.

I imagined escaping from wretched beasts to arrive at the late Cretaceous Period about 75 million years ago. Those frightening beasts hadn't yet left the scene, but now a great inland sea lapped the shore with tidal ripples in the mud covered by seaweed. The air remained heavy with no mountain breezes—just a flat swamp with bright, green-eyed iguanodons pitter-pattering along the mud in search of lush, fern-like cycads. Gigantic feathered beasts flapped their awkward wings above my head and cackled like mythological harpies. The tan, dark gray, and black shales oozed with mud and slime. I see that Mini has stepped into a mud puddle, and once again I hear the roar of i-70.

What I like most about Dinosaur Ridge is the relative peace and calm on top of its rocky spine. Up there grow yuccas, cacti, Gambel oak, pinyon pine, Utah juniper, sagebrush, mountain mahogany, kinnikinnick, golden banner, harebells, and scores of other wildflowers. Sailing overhead are ravens, hawks, golden eagles, and swallows. Nearby are buzzing hummingbirds. Mini, a ground -level cocker spaniel, simply loves it up here on the ridge between September and April, when there are no snakes to worry about. She loves to peer over the edge of cliffs and stare into space. All I have to say is "go see!" and she runs to the edge and takes it all in. She stops and listens to chickadees going chick-a-dee-dee-dee. She eyeballs each pine squirrel scampering up a twisted tree trunk. Even when she squats to urinate, she's all eyes for what's going on around her. Yes, she's a worthy successor to the dinosaurs of old.

At a certain narrow point on the trail's crest, I often stop and feel the texture of a rock, rippled and uplifted from that inland sea of millions of years ago. Algal materials covered earlier ripples and preserved their form when beaches became buried under layers of other deposits that hardened to rock. Tidal ripples are amazing to behold millions of years later—more amazing, in a sense, than the sarcophagus of the Emperor Charlemagne, or the Rosetta Stone. Why? Sixty million years! Imagine finding a 60-million-year-old plant in your backyard. How can one fathom the meaning of a wilderness of time found in 60million years? A sand ripple is as common on the receded sea delta of the Colorado River down in Mexico as it was on the Great Inland Sea of ancient interior Colorado. But 60 million years separate the two ripples. Ripples we can understand, but the time between may be impossible. Or is it? We do have that special gift of Kantian intuition and Thoreauvian imagination. Dreams can cut through time like lightning through clouds to illuminate an otherwise darkened land. A stegosaur's roar and thumping step can still be heard in the spirit's core. The numbers sixty, 60 million, and 60 billion do not defy the human spirit. We can even imagine various species of dinosaurs having green flesh with orange spots.

I remember driving up i-70one extremely windy day to an early January conference site on Lookout Mountain above Denver. Flames raced up the northeast slope of Dinosaur Ridge. Pinyon trees blazed with sparks that hopped up the ridge in a spectacle of beauty and terror. The blackened vegetation below the flames stood phantom like in marked contrast to the whiteness of snow. Within days of my conference, Mini and I walked along that ridge top to inspect the damage. Mini sniffed the air and ground full-time once we arrived at darkened soil and blackened pine branches. Even snow had become dark with black and gray ashes, making for fertile soil next spring. Not too much damage here.

One mild February weekend we had a surprise visit from our son. My wife Maura and I packed a lunch for the three of us, with treats for Mini, to take advantage of the warm, pre-spring sunshine up on Dinosaur Ridge. Buds laced the branches of bare scrub oaks, and the most delicate and tiny flowers of sandworts graced the ground at our feet like miniature dots of snow. Arriving at a high sandstone upthrust, we stopped for lunch. The foothills of the Rockies spread westward and upward, obscuring the high Front Range. We could clearly see that our ridge protruded skyward as an uneroded shell fragment of an outer layer of sandstone and shale that once covered the Rocky Mountains. We finished our lunch atop the layers of time by recollecting our own family layers of time when Rich was a boy in Laramie with his two sisters, Michelle and Maureen. We all had a good reunion up there on the ridge. Rich now lived in Seattle and his sisters in New York and Fort Lauderdale—as spread apart as sediment from the Rockies that had traveled down prairie streams to the sea.

One crisp autumn day I hiked solo over the ridge when oak leaves had changed to bright scarlet. They rustled like prayer flags in the Himalayas. High in the foothills across the way, tongues of aspen blazed with a golden fire. Gray clouds swooped upslope like volcanic clouds millions of years ago when tectonic plates collided within the Laramide Orogeny. During our civilized state, we humans have experienced very little volcanism. Vesuvius, Etna, Krakatoa, and Mount Saint Helens were tiny firecrackers compared to the eruptions of the Yellowstone Caldera 600,000 years ago, when our primitive continent lay blackened for months on end. How frightening it must have been to see ranges of volcanoes puffing and exploding red-hot lava.

Snow sprinkled down from the upsloping clouds and gathered in windy wisps along my trail. A yellow-jacket bee buzzed for cover among the last of the autumnal flowers still barely in bloom. It snowed yet harder in chilling winds, and the sky darkened. It felt good to be up here; I could have easily been hundreds of miles away. It grew even colder, and some leaves blew off the scrub oaks. My hands and feet grew numb, and it was time to make my descent to the cares of the city below. Chickadees along the trail chirped to bid me farewell.

Yes, I'm glad I discovered a place called Dinosaur Ridge. Up there, my urban-encased being is truly energized and revitalized. It is a place of magic—magical realism. It is a place that allows the spirit to roam free through time and space.

Sun Dance Notes

Merrill Gilfillan
from *Rivers and Birds*

*It is hard to think of a more patient and perceptive observer of the
West's lonely stretches than essayist and poet Merrill Gilfillan.
In this piece the author, standing on the edge of another culture,
shares his notes on "what men and women did on earth today."*

1. Arapaho

The grounds lie in a large open field just east of Ethete, Wyoming.
The Wind River range rises to the west. The camp surrounding the
sun lodge is a big one with many white tepees among the smaller
tents and occasional trailers. Each family camp has erected three-
sided sun- and windbreaks of willow boughs lashed onto stalls of
poles and boards.

The Northern Arapaho sun dance is esteemed as one of the purest
of sun dances. There are guests from all over the West, including a
sizable contingent from Oklahoma: Kiowas and of course Southern
Arapahos visiting kin in Wyoming. This being Sunday, the final day
of the gathering, there are other visitors stopping by. A local priest in
black robes and a panama hat stands chatting with friends. A handsome Arapaho girl carrying a large cudgel checks my daypack for
camera or recorder.

The chorus of eagle-bone whistles and drum is steady from inside
the sun lodge. The aroma of sage pervades the July day. Stacks of fresh-
cut reeds for the dancers' resting beds wait near the entryway. Elders
in lawn chairs watch every move within with alert but not laborious
attention. One old man cries out occasionally, exhorting the dancers.

The Southern Arapaho women stand out in their attire and carriage. The older ones are dressed up in an unmistakable, pre-World
War II Southern way that both defies and diminishes the afternoon

heat. They wear fancy floral dresses and seamed stockings and permed coiffures with hairnets over them and carry bright parasols. Their sweet accents and laughter drift through the camp.

After several hours the near-constant tooting of the bone whistles becomes a feature of the very day, irrepressible, like August crickets. As afternoon breaks and the final evening of dancing begins, the intensity of dancers, singers, even onlookers heightens subtly.

Gulls sail continually over the lodge, crying, tacking, casting an eye. *What men and women did on the continent today. July 1987.*

2. Cheyenne

A high, level meadow enclosed by ponderosa pines, twelve miles south of Lame Deer. The slowly growing camp of tents encircles the glade, hugs the edge of the cooling pines. Mountain bluebirds and crossbills call.

Friday morning: The camp crier on his bay horse rides through camp, publicly summoning members of various men's societies. A dozen of them eventually gather in the middle of the glade and confer, then slowly begin to lay out the sun lodge site, marking it off and soon setting the forked cottonwood uprights with posthole diggers and crowbars.

There is something engaging in the lopped, leafy cotton wood limbs laid out at the ready on the ground nearby—a compelling image, the idea of a simple common thing cut and handled with ritual care and concern. The stack of them lies there, half wild, half sanctified, leaves still twinkling in the piney breeze.

Camp sounds gradually intensify: wood being chopped, children at play. Latter afternoon, the crier on his bay horse drags the central sun pole into the skeleton of the lodge; the walls of cottonwood boughs are up. It is complete. Essentially, a handful of men from the societies do it all, sustain the details of it all through the generations Friday evening: Suddenly the devotees emerge from the Lone Tepee. Wrapped in blankets or buffalo robes, they proceed slowly, s topping and starting in traditional ritual hesitance. Abraham Spotted Elk directs, quietly and surely. The camp bustle subsides a bit. Then for thirty minutes they circle the lodge in the prescribed formal manner of entry, moving slowly, with their advisers/"grandfathers" at their sides, as the sky takes on a pinkish sundown cast.

The pace is snail slow, with endless consulting between Abraham and his assistants: low talk and pointing, looking around. It has taken all day to raise the sun lodge and get the dancers properly inside, and now the process of trans formation is well under way. A pleasant glade in the pine woods is steadily transformed into a holy place with the lodge as its sanctified center. The alteration is accomplished through steady, infinitely patient codified action of endless detail, work whose materials are earth, cherry sticks, cotton wood limbs, the bone of skull. The most daily of things, garnered and shifted to the sacred.

The camp life and its social sounds comprise a major component of the experience, provide the context that gives the event its public relevance and resonance. The laughter, the squall of children, the cooking smoke from many fires, the racks of sliced meat drying at each camp-site, the constant coming and going of low-slung cars and pickups. There are license plates from Oklahoma, Arizona, Wyoming. It is all utterly casual around the camp. Cars honk and teenagers crack wise. Small children are left to their own devices; there is no effort made to impress them with the religious significance of the gathering, though they are occasionally hushed at important moments in the lodge proceedings. Amid this, when there is something to announce, the crier makes his rounds on his bay horse with a far-carrying baritone "Heeeyeey! Heeey-eey!" and proclaims the news in Cheyenne.

Throughout Saturday the transformation builds. The dancers are fully painted and dancing; the eagle whistles pulse all day; the mud-hole around the water pump deepens. And by evening, when the inner lodge is illuminated by fire light, the sense of circumscribed sanctum is full: the marked-off, carefully created sanctum. The interior of the lodge—the cottonwood beams, the dancers' willow-bough rest-beds, the shadows moving on the walls—is altered after just a day and a half. The sage on the floor is trampled. It has the feel of a long-occupied, comfortable, receptive place.

The sun dance songs have a hymn-like harmony. Many of them begin very softly, build caressingly, to finally kick in, the eagle whistles joining. I fall asleep to them rising and falling, seventy-five yards away. Sunday daybreak: The dancers gather at the eastern door way of the lodge to dance as the sun rises. Abraham prays silently beside them. The tribal and the American flags flap from a tepee pole. The first sun strikes the inner altar, its buffalo skull, rows of chokecherry sticks, rows of leafy branches stuck in the ground.

Late afternoon: Five dancers go through the piercing: wooden skewers thrust through the skin of the chest and attached with a hide rope to the sun pole or to a heavy buffalo skull. There is gooseflesh through the crowd of onlookers as the struggle to break free begins. After, a man sobs as he em braces one of the piercers in the lowering sunlight.

What people did on the earth today. August 1988

For a week following, I held the pace of that patient, generation-after-generation procedure, the measure of distilled Knowing Motion. And heard remnants of the gentler sun dance songs in my head. And weeks after, I heard the crier's mellow public exhortatory voice, the calling to attention—"heeey-eey." Re sorted to it on occasion during solitary walks on the prairie, used it when saluting a surprise coulee, a change in the wind, a sudden flock of larks.

3. Blackfoot

The camp is set in a mile-wide swale between Highway 2 and the railroad tracks, four miles east of Browning. A long crescent drainage-ditch mound lends privacy on the south, the highway side where big trucks roll. The swale is bright green after a wet spring, flecked with flowers. The outer most peaks of Glacier Park are just visible to the northwest.

The camp of dome tents, pickup campers, and vans en circles the Lone Tepee and the open site where the sun lodge will be raised. Three skeletal sun lodge frames from former years stand to the west of camp in various stages of weathering; a few faded offering cloths still toss in the breeze. Pickup trucks come and go with loads of firewood and port-a-johns. One unloads a four-hundred-gallon U.S. Marine Corps water caisson.

A long westbound freight train passes on the northern edge of the grounds, a short half mile from the camp. Meadowlarks and upland plovers sing in the evening sun. The pledger and leaders of the sun dance enter the Lone Tepee for the final night of preparatory singing. Another freight train rolls through. The engineer leans on his el bows at the window of the Burlington Northern engine, checking out the activity—seems to slow a bit. Darkness finally falls at 10 o'clock.

The next morning is cloudy and drizzly, a strong northern odor of alder on the air. A pair of ferruginous hawks is nesting, remarkably, in the upper forks of last year's sun lodge, not far from the new site. One of them frequently sails above the grounds, crying. The people are quietly honored, refer to them as "the eagles." Cars and vans arrive continually: New Mexico, Saskatchewan, Wyoming, Alberta plates. Tepees go up; people are busy preparing sage crown-wreaths and wristlets with red felt wrappings for the dancers.

At midday the sun lodge is marked off with seven-foot aspens stuck in the earth. The outer frame poles have been cut and lie in a rough circle at the perimeter. By mid-afternoon participants and their families begin to dress. Others test their eagle whistles, blending with the hawks' cries.

Then a large truck pulls in with the sacred center (sun) pole and rafters. They drive in quickly and unload. The sun pole is set with its upper end at rest on a tripod. Four pick ups unload piles of aspen boughs: again, that uncanny flash of the wild everyday thing in all its latency, on the verge of transmogrification.

By early evening, all is set, at the ready in a deep stillness. An hour later men are called from the camp and the pole is raised as Buster Yellow Kidney prays beside. There is the intermittent crackle of pre-July Fourth fireworks from dwellings off beyond the highway. Later in the evening, the dancers enter the completed lodge.

The following day the dancing is in full session, the whistles' throbbing soon a part of the morning. The songs seem to be "inter-tribal": Some are Blackfoot, they say; many are Canadian Cree.

I drive into Browning once or twice a day for food. Some people in town speak in scattered snatches of the sun dance, some challenging its integrity and pastiche style, particularly the number of women and Caucasian dancers (there is a contingent from Chicago, fans of Buster Yellow Kidney). . . .

During the day I develop a simple pattern as observer. I stand near the sun lodge entrance for a while, watching the dancers at close hand. Women on one side of the lodge, men on the other. Then I wander off to put some distance on it, take my lawn chair off into the swale to sit alone, or climb the rise just north of the camp and sit there among the swaying flowers and wild roses for an hour. The camp is very lovely from that knoll, spread in afternoon sun, and the sun lodge especially has a great tender beauty from afar, its sloping walls of twelve-foot aspens shimmering in that semisecular, consecrated glow.

Mid-afternoon the piercing begins. Three men, and then three women, their friends at their sides with tears in their eyes. Silent older men are there to advise, catch the piercers as they break free from the ropes.

After that the peace of early evening is calming. There is a buoyant meadow lull. A soft wind buffets the grasses. Pipits and vesper sparrows sing during the quiet of the sup per hour. Against the soft sky to the west, the hawks stand out in silhouette on the old sun lodge, the adults hunch backed and blinking in the rafters, a single woolly young one gaping foul-breathed in the nest.

I stroll up to my favorite knoll and sit on the ground. Smoke from cook fires rises above camp. In a few minutes a seven-year-old girl walks up the slope and presents me shyly with a pork chop and two slices of white bread on a paper plate, a gift from her parents to a visitor, a lingering guest.

At intervals dancers leave the sanctum to walk slowly, their heads covered with blankets, to the pit toilets just east of camp, each accompanied by a helper. They line up and wait their turn silently on the rise.

I finish my pork chop and decide to take a walk, across the meadow to the railroad tracks. There I sit beside a willow clump and smoke, and weep for a minute, and smoke again, amid the pretty yarrow and red-eyed susans and horse droppings.

I hear the eagle whistles begin again from the distant lodge. If prayer rises, this must be something like the sun hears. Then a big westbound train goes through, loaded piggyback with Hanjin and Mitsui freight cars.

What men and women did on the earth today. June 1990

I Used to Stomp on Grasshoppers

Chip Ward
from *Hope's Horizon: Three Visions
for Healing the American Land*

*Chip Ward profiles a range of environmental activists
across the county. Here he describes a personal epiphany,
an awakening to the diversity and inter-relatedness of
the natural world embodied in such activism.*

I used to stomp on grasshoppers. Any chance I got. If one crossed my path on a country road or a sidewalk, I would heel-hunt it into the ground. Bam-splat! Another one bites the dust. My dislike of grasshoppers was active, violent, and righteous. I was a god, walking this earth and dispensing life-or-death judgments on the lowly creatures that crawled and jumped beneath my feet.

The animosity and contempt I felt toward grasshoppers was the result of personal experience. Since moving to Utah's West Desert more than two decades ago, I have experienced two grasshopper infestations. An infestation, or plague as it is commonly called, must be experienced to be appreciated. I have seen groves of trees in summer stripped down to their winter profiles by a million tiny relentless jaws. I have seen gray, weathered fenceposts gnawed down to raw blond wood when swarms of hoppers ran out of vegetation to chew on. I have driven roads cobbled with their carcasses. I once drove over a flood of grasshoppers making their way from a field they had reduced to stubble to fresh food on the other side of the road. As I drove over them, they leaped by the thousands, hitting the bottom of the truck and making the rattling cacophony of an upside-down hailstorm.

What I have experienced, though, was nothing compared to the plagues of the past, like the swarm of locusts that crossed the Great

Plains into Colorado in 1875. That year, Rocky Mountain locusts became a kind of superorganism of metabolic wildfire more than 100 miles wide and 1,800 miles long that eclipsed the sun and gleaned a whole landscape down to bristles and dust. Settlers reported that the insects even ate the wool off living sheep.

Though not historic in scale, my experiences were nonetheless powerful. I can vividly recall tiptoeing, arms crossed protectively around my body, through a field of long, slender stems that were bent and trembling with the weight of grasshoppers lined up head to tail along their lengths. Halfway across, I was overcome by nausea. The grasshoppers were voracious. Prolific. Creepy. Once you have lived through their plague, you do not hold much affection for these insects or appreciate their return. One less grasshopper, in my book, was a welcome development. And so I stomped on them.

Oysters made me stop. I can explain. Some years ago I came across a remarkable account of oyster behavior in an essay, "High Tide in Tucson," by Barbara Kingsolver. A scientist named F. A. Brown collected some oyster specimens along the Connecticut shoreline for research he was doing on the cycles of intertidal oysters. He took his little prisoners to a basement lab in landlocked Illinois. For the first couple of weeks in their new time zone, the oysters kept their Atlantic coast schedule. As the tide was rolling into Connecticut, they would open up in unison to feed on the briny plankton they expected to arrive. As the tide in Connecticut rolled out, they would shut tight and wait for the next tide. This, after all, was the pattern of their prespecimen lives, and one that was kept for eons by their clammy ancestors. Then, over the next two weeks, an unexpected shift occurred. By the end of that time the oysters were still following a tidal pattern, but not on a schedule charted by man or woman. What was going on? Brown and his students crunched some numbers and made a startling discovery. The oysters were in perfect sync with what the Atlantic tides' schedule would have been had they pushed on beyond Connecticut, across the length of New York state, over the Midwest and eventually rolled into the oysters' Chicago basement lab.

Think about it. First, it's remarkable that these ancient and brainless slips of simple salty flesh, with no eyes, ears, or voices, could do anything in unison that was not the result of some heavy-duty simultaneous outside stimulation, like hooking a car battery to their aquarium and throwing the switch. To Brown and his colleagues, who were familiar with the myriad ways that plants, animals, and insects communicate and coordinate through hormones and other chemicals, the oysters' ability to act in unison was not surprising. But it was amazing that they somehow managed to anticipate a distant and subtle planetary rhythm without benefit of cues from the sun, moon, or stars, let alone the powerful moving ocean waters that had sustained their slow beat until they were captured and shipped away. How did they do it? What atmospheric, geologic, or biologic music do they dance to that we humans, with all our high-tech calculating capacity, cannot fathom?

Kingsolver's essay made me rethink my relationship with grass hoppers (and just about everything else). Grasshoppers, it seems to me, are potentially far more sophisticated than oysters. What do they know that I don't? Maybe the ebb and flow of their population is a response to some subtle planetary shift that I, in my blind and righteous sophistication, am not able to discern.

I began to take a second look. One of the first things I learned is that my original opinion of grasshoppers is not universally shared. Certainly not by the conservation biologists I encountered on my journey, who taught me about the intrinsic value of all species, the mysteries and wonders of ecological processes we do not fully comprehend, and the value and role of natural "disturbances" like fire and flood. My "kill the pest" attitude was similar to the approach we have followed when wiping out predators. It was not the least biocentric. So I stepped back and tried to see grasshoppers from the different perspective I had been learning.

How would those grasshoppers look to a bird? Mighty good. Our plague is their feast and fortune. Skunks, too, see it differently. Although I have some serious questions about the value and purpose of skunks in the grand scheme of life—again because I have had several negative experiences with that species, including getting sprayed twice—I am quite fond of birds. They animate the landscape, embroider the sky, and fill my mornings with song. I envy their ability to swoop and soar. In the winter, I find myself searching the horizon for twirling ribbons of starlings, awed by their collective tubular dance, the choreography of undulating columns of black birds. I look in shrubs for the tiny seedeaters that remain behind while others have migrated far and wide. I watch them huddle, hop, and peck. I miss their singing cousins and long for their return in the spring.

Birds, of course, are valuable not just for the aesthetic pleasures they bring. They are important as pollinators, and pollinators make life on earth possible. Also, by carrying undigested seeds in their droppings, they are important as seed distributors. Birds, you could say, are teamsters of biodiversity—each poop a Peterbilt.

As any HawkWatch member with a pair of binoculars can tell you, birds are also significant indicators of the health of the environment. Just as canaries in coal mines warned miners of the presence of dangerous fumes, birds give us an early warning of other environmental dangers. In the year following the Chernobyl disaster, for example, a precipitous decline in songbird populations in North America and Europe offered powerful evidence of how far radiation from Chernobyl had reached and the potent effect it had. The absence of bird song that year was not just a sensual deprivation, it was a powerful message that we are all downwind and downstream from one another.

Birds don't just work and warn; they also reveal. As any bird-watcher knows, to do it right you must slow down, be still, and look and listen intently. You must understand habitat and learn the principles of wind and weather, climate, and seasons. You must tune in to behaviors that are rooted in cycles of mating, nesting, growth, and migration. In other words, to find and know birds, you must learn the primal, nonhuman language of life. Ask bird-watchers why they do it and they will likely describe the peaceful and reflective aspects of birding: how it can be a tonic for the mind and spirit in an age of stress and striving. They can tell you about moving lessons they have learned from birds—lessons about life and about how to simply be. I find it ironic that today's popular culture is so obsessed with angels with wings who look like us, while we ignore the winged creatures who surround us, already here and available to guide us to peace and understanding. But these angels eat grasshoppers. If I am so fond of birds, I reasoned, then maybe I should be more tolerant of their food.

Being attentive is key. The more I learn about the intricacies of food webs and nutrient cycles, the more I appreciate how every plant, animal, and insect, even the lowly bacteria, can play an essential role in some life process we humans do not fully understand or appreciate. An entomologist I know is fond of reminding his less bug oriented friends that we are utterly dependent on life processes that bacteria and bugs contribute to in important ways. Beetles, he loves to point out, could exist very well without humans, but humans, who are dependent on soil that beetles help build and process, could not exist without beetles. Al though life's individual threads may seem insignificant, pull anyone of them and you cannot be sure what will unravel and how the consequences will be magnified as they travel along the tapestry of being.

I always knew that stomping on grasshoppers was petty and foolish behavior. Now, in the light of my attempt to understand conservation biology, I have to admit it is also arrogant. Who am I to judge the value and purpose of grasshoppers? What do I know about the natural cycles that underlie their rise and fall? The way a landscape consumes itself, shits itself out, reseeds, and starts over is often a matter of disturbance and even catastrophe. The specific conditions and chemical signals that push grasshoppers, crickets, and locusts into all consuming migration are not well understood. The thinking that prevails today is that drought causes populations to crowd together for scant food. Proximity triggers chemical signals that lead to hyped-up breeding, and increased breeding leads to faster consumption of available food, thus compelling migration in search of new food. At some point, physiological changes appear. Wings lengthen for extended flight. Although I cannot see the tipping point where micro changes become mega, I should at least be able to recognize an ecological process when I see it, even if it is not appealing.

Fires and floods are two other ecological processes that have gotten a bad reputation because their opening acts are so clearly destructive. The changes and exchanges in nutrients they kick off are more subtle, slower, and harder to perceive. Perhaps rampaging hoppers also have hidden functions.

I do not have a firm handle on the mystery of how life on earth unfolds and keeps its dynamic balance while perched on the edge of chaos. I can't be sure exactly how I fit into the larger patterns that sustain me or the role that grasshoppers and oysters play in that pattern that connects one to all. As Reed Noss argues, life on earth expresses an intelligence and underlying order that is too complex for us to fully grasp, try as we may. Maybe a little humility is in order.

We are of this world—"dust to dust," as they say. Before we acquired the cultural habit of capturing our moldering flesh behind teakwood and oak six feet under, our bodily fate was to be fodder for the juice and sinew of a world that lived on after our demise. Just as we now refuse to blend in the end, we also deny the utter rootedness of our lives in a wide world that loops through us and feeds back to us in an intricate weave too complex to fathom.

Fact one: we are embedded in this world. Although we are, and should be, recognized for our unique human abilities, from writing symphonies to traveling to the moon, it is also fair to say that we are what we eat, what we drink, and what we breathe. Again, if you stop eating for three weeks, stop taking in fluids for three days, or stop breathing for three minutes, your body will make the case for you that the process of life is the constant transformation of environment into physical being.

The food we eat is a synthesis of water, sunlight, and soil. Soil is the rich mix of plant debris, bits of sand and stone, and the decomposing flesh of every living thing you can name as it is consumed and trans formed by communities of worms, insects, and microbes. A microbial world we barely know hums through us. An acre of soil includes ten tons of microbial and invertebrate life, the weight equivalent of ten Clydesdale draft horses, galloping not overland but underground.

We are also fluid creatures. Our blood tosses the salt of seas. Tears, amniotic fluid, sweat, piss, and our vulnerable wet flesh from head to toe contain whatever is carried in the currents, storms, and tides that sweep the globe and in the streams and rivers that drain the rain and snow. The same breeze that lifts the wings of birds also fills your lungs. Our continual biological communion with the planet is undeniable and profound.

Once the direct pathways between the biosphere and our own blood and bones become clear, the health of the land should become a self-evident concern of self-interest. If biodiversity is a key to planetary health, as conservation biologists attest, then biodiversity should be come a measure of the success and well-being of humans that is as significant and important as the gross national product. Life's buzzing, blooming, and howling variability—from caribou to cactus, from marigolds to loons, from mussels to moss—makes life viable. To the ex tent that we damage that robust diversity, we are engaged in self-destructive and unsustainable behaviors because we are connected to what we are destroying. If we chop it up, it dies and eventually so do we, or we limp along in a diminished and dysfunctional world. Paradoxically, it is in our self-interest to be selfless and generous, for the health of the world is ultimately our own.

We know how to make the land pay—how the land can make wealth. We do not know how the land makes health. That requires a different language than the one we are adept at using. That new language of health, the one that conservation biologists are trying to invent, will be a challenge to acquire because it differs radically from the language of wealth. Wealth says more, health says enough. Wealth says accumulate, health says flow. Wealth says compete and win, while health says reciprocate, integrate, and reconcile. Wealth says manage and measure, health says jam and dance. Wealth assigns value, health assumes it. Wealth adds, subtracts, and divides. Health makes whole.

Yes, wealth is needed and can certainly be good and welcome. I enjoy my comforts. I am glad I do not hunger. I like being entertained. People across the globe have indisputable material needs that are not being met. But common sense and wisdom tell us that health is the ultimate bottom line. Rich soils, benign weather, breathing forests, filtering wet lands, clean freshwater, and abundant seas are hard to quantify and measure for the very reason that they are so important and valuable. "In calculable" is the word to describe their worth.

After sacrificing environmental health for profits, power, jobs, and revenue that benefits a relative handful of the world's people for hundreds of years, it is time to restore the balance. Time to end the imbalance of power that strives to lock in the obscenely unequal distribution of wealth which allows a small elite to grow ever richer while a massive population struggles and suffers for a fraction of the rewards from their own labor and lands. Across the globe, the landless poor slash and burn, strip the land of trees for fuel, deplete soils, and poach wild game until they are forced to flee into crowded urban slums, where they sell their labor for slave wages and succumb to tainted water and food. Ecological destruction and social injustice are twin engines of global corporate capitalism as it is currently configured.

Time also to restore the balance of our minds. We cannot find the courage and creativity to address the central imbalance while holding on to the attitudes, assumptions, and beliefs that are so closely related to the very problems compelling our attention. This is not a matter of adopting a new ideology, although we will certainly be challenging a prevailing worldview if we challenge the criteria that underlie our cur rent policies and choices. It is more a matter of learning by doing differently. Today we provide kids with lots of opportunities to compute, compete, keep score, accumulate, manipulate, and fix. We do not normally give them chances to contemplate, compost, and plant. Every legislator I know wants a computer in every classroom. I have yet to meet one who thinks each classroom should have its own garden. Being able to balance the books is a required skill. Bird watching and bulb planting are optional.

Sue Morse, John Derick, Howard Gross, Michael Soulé, Leanne Klyza Linck, Kim Vacariu, Jim Catlin, Allison Jones, Tom Butler, and many others I have encountered over the past few years are gaining and sharing understandings about how the natural world connects, communicates, and creates. Cutting off feedback loops when we don't know the role they play or the impacts of losing them, reducing the pool of possibilities and weakening a living system's resilience, and introducing alien variables are all reckless and risky practices.

The work of understanding the health of whole ecosystems and reweaving the broken strands is the way we learn to survive our own mistakes. It will point toward ways of living more lightly on the land. It may open new ways to converse with nature and create new languages, maps, and lenses. That work is the seedbed of a new culture focused on diverse, restored, and robust nature that will, like the ecosystems it seeks to heal, emerge and self-organize from the seeds we sow.

The dilemma for those of us trying to carve a new paradigm for our times is that philosophy does not precede perception. Like a well honed nose and a universe of rich aromas, belief and perception call each other into being. How do you describe harmony and wholeness, their value and necessity, when the world around you is cacophonous, splintered, and dissonant? Healing and "rewilding" wounded lands, then, is not only the way we ensure our own physical vitality and sanity, it is the way we can learn the hard work of reconnection.

Reconnect the land. Reconnect our bodies to the land. Reconnect body and spirit.

We will need places to learn how to do that work, and there are prob ably no pristine places left. Early Amerindians wiped out mastodons, and their descendants used fire as a tool to shape grass-lands and forests to their needs. They irrigated, built villages, cut woods, and otherwise left their indelible marks, though certainly on a scale that pales next to our own impact. As island biogeographers show us, even the wildest places we have agreed to protect are islands withering from isolation and disconnection with the larger land-scapes that once included them.

But large tracts of land with integrity and diverse life, the surest sign of health and the potential for resilience, do remain. Even in the crowded East, fragments of wildlands are often close to one another, begging for attention and reconnection into whole systems. Saving wilderness and near-wilderness provides us with places to start, learn, and practice how to help the earth's own healing powers take hold.

Health is the natural state of living systems that are allowed to function with integrity over time. That is what I have learned. It is right to honor Nature and wise to heed her. To stay healthy, we must be humble.

I used to stomp on grasshoppers. Oysters made me stop.

6 ✹ Seeking Balance

This final section of The Landscape of Home *offers a kind of summary and charge, bringing together and highlighting what we have seen here and there throughout this book, some of the core and continuing controversies about our presence and effects on this land. Although it is not easy to figure out how to earn our livings in the West while at the same time protecting and preserving everything we love most about it, this is a goal we share, a task worthy of our best efforts.*

Oh, Canada

Frank Clifford
from *The Backbone of the World:*
A Portrait of the Vanishing West
along the Continental Divide

Frank Clifford traveled the length of the Continental Divide in
writing this book. Here he takes the reader to one of the last
best places, telling of one person's quixotic attempts to halt its
wholesale destruction in the drive for profit.

"So he's going with crazy Mike, eh?"

The words drift across the wooden counters in the Beaver Mines general store where I am picking up supplies for a pack trip into the Canadian Rockies. I am going with Mike Judd, a former cow boy and hunting guide, best known lately for his acts of defiance against the oil and gas industry. A year ago, he was confined to the county mental hospital after he made off with a Caterpillar and threatened to tear up a road that Shell/Canada had built in one of the last unspoiled canyons in southern Alberta's Castle-Crown Wilderness.

I look over at the four men joking in the front of the store, one of them jerking a thumb in my direction. "You think he knows what he's in for?"

When I was growing up in Minnesota, Canada beckoned like Atlantis. It was a boy's world, right out of the fictional wilderness I had immersed myself in—Kenneth Roberts's Northwest Passage and novelist Joseph Altsheler's tales of a band of daring frontier lads pad dling silently across indigo lakes and sleeping on the forest floor. In my eyes Canada was all forest and indigo lakes. I went with my father almost every August. It took us all day to reach the border, a slow, hot drive past farm fields and lakeside tourist courts with their riot of homemade billboards hawking night crawlers and all-you-can-eat crappie suppers. The clutter disappeared when we crossed into Canada at Lake of the Woods. My father referred to the country north of the border as the Canadian Shield. It is the name geologists gave to the nucleus of the continent, the first part of North America to rise permanently above sea level. For me, it was the great granite battlement beyond which all familiar trappings and responsibilities dropped away and the realm of summer began. The forest massed in front of us. A breeze rose off the water. The air smelled like gin, my father said.

"I don't want to disappoint you," Mike Judd says to me as we climb into his truck and head for his horse camp on the South Castle River. "I'm afraid you're going to find that this isn't the Canada of your youth. The oil companies, the timber companies, the cattle ranchers . . . they've all had their way with this country, and it shows it."

But this trip isn't just about Canada. It is my last stop, a time of reckoning. I had gone from border to border and a bit beyond, spent the better part of two years exploring an endangered landscape. I had listened to the arguments about why it was so and who was to blame. The world of the Divide was animated by feuds—between cowboys and conservationists, sheepherders and coyotes, wolves and elk—and it would be a lesser place for the loss of any of the antagonists. Its appeal comes not only from mountain meadows and sculpted canyons, but from the relics of history—the bones of homesteads, the names of immigrant herders carved in aspen bark—and from the sinuous architecture of broken country, whether shaped by wind and drought, by a miner's dynamite or a rancher's cows. If there is a common element to it all, it is threadbare grace. You see it in the desert bighorn that goes without water for six months or the shepherd who supports a family on $5,000 a year. The West that captures the imagination is often an impoverished landscape, poor in moisture and nourishment, exposed and distressed, worn to burnished bedrock. Yet, it is possible to get carried away with graveyard aesthetics, like Shelley's desert traveler contemplating the majestic wreckage of Ozymandias and its inscription: Look on my works, ye mighty, and despair.

Mike Judd does not encourage such thinking. He is not ready to accept the role that society has scripted for him, as a refugee from the nineteenth century or an expatriate from the wilderness. "I'm going to show you the good, the bad, and the ugly," he says. "And when you've seen it, I hope you'll want to do something about it."

I had heard about Mike from environmentalists in the United States. They called him a cowboy Cassandra, a prophet of ecological ruin, ignored in his own country. A scold to neighbors and a worry to his family, he had eventually taken his message south of the border, where he found a more responsive audience. Five years ago, his warnings about the industrialization of wilderness along the Continental Divide helped persuade U.S. Forest Service officials in Montana to put a chunk of the northern Rocky Mountains off-limits to logging, mining, and oil drilling.

Canada hadn't weakened its environmental policies since I was a boy. It just hadn't seen the need to pass strict laws. There was so much country, bigger than the United States, even counting Alaska, and so much of it unspoiled. The first paved cross-country highway wasn't finished until the 1960s. Even after Canada became a force in international timber and energy markets, and the Western provinces began to exhibit scars that did not heal, there was no push for wilderness preservation comparable to U.S. efforts. Indeed, the absence of such laws has given Canadian companies a competitive advantage. For example, by the year 2000, they were meeting about 35 percent of the U.S. timber demand. They are not about to trade market share for stronger environmental protection. Meanwhile, the Ministry of Environment dutifully looks for ways to protect Canada's endangered species, which now number around 300, but can't come up with a law that provincial politicians will agree to. All of Canada's provinces have gained power over the past thirty years as the central government in Ottawa sought to placate separatists in Quebec. As a result, it has become increasingly difficult for the federal government to exert authority on any number of issues. Eventually, Canada's inaction on the environment is bound to have repercussions.

"It'll affect you guys in the lower forty-eight," Mike says to me. "Our wildlife is your wildlife. They don't stop at the border. A lot of them—the bears and the wolves, mainly—come from up here. If we stop growing them, you'll stop seeing them."

Mike steers his truck up a rough gravel road toward his camp. The old Ford rides low and slow, piled high with saddles, panniers, and boxes of frozen food and portable kitchen equipment. His three-year-old husky, Keeper, sits between us in the cab alongside his 12-gauge, his copy of *The Gulag Archipelago,* and a bullwhip he uses to chase the neighbors' cows out of riverside vegetation. "If they have their way, they'll eat all the grass along the river. If I have mine, they'll go out a little thinner than when they come in."

Just past fifty, Mike is slight and wiry, with a grizzled face and eyes that twinkle and fade. He grew up on his father's small ranch, rode a horse to school in Pincher Creek, finished the twelfth grade, and lit out across the mountains for a job with the biggest cattle operation in British Columbia. He returned after five years to help his brother run the family's ranch and start a wilderness-outfitting business. But southern Alberta was changing. The wilderness was being fragmented and the game scattered. You could drive a pickup into places that not that long ago were accessible only by horse or a mule. The changes weighed heavily on Mike. He withdrew from the company of the cowboys, roughnecks, and loggers whose colorful society he had craved as a boy. "Every time an issue of conservation came along, they were on the other side. That was not helpful to me because as a guide my living depended on these mountains. I tried to point out the value of leaving them alone, but the more I did that, the more I became an alien."

The first gas wells were drilled in 1902 inside the boundaries of what is now Waterton Lakes National Park, just north of the Montana border. Today, there isn't a major valley for fifty miles north of Waterton without an access road servicing a well, a pipeline, or a processing plant. Nearly 300 miles of roads have been built into the narrow canyons that run perpendicular to the spine of the Rockies. Most of them dead-end against the flanks of the Divide, where Mike and I are headed. Half of the elk habitat has been destroyed in the mountains around Pincher Creek and Waterton. Less than a quarter of the grizzly bear's home range is still intact. Its numbers have declined by more than 90 percent over the past century. Biologists predict southern Alberta will be the next place where they go extinct.

The human population of southern Alberta is deceptively sparse. It is an unhurried, uncluttered place of tidy, clapboard towns, English gardens, and a sea of green hills lapping against the mountains that float in the distance like gray-barnacled leviathans. Words like "nice" and "just so" come to mind when describing the bright red window boxes plump with geraniums or the wooden door knockers in the form of a hand-painted Canada goose. To a lot of people, the term "wild" is a pejorative, something to be washed out of the dog's fur like skunk odor. It brings to mind the "black wind" that rakes these hills in the winter or the thin, stony soil that broke the spirits of the North Dakota farmers who thought they were coming to an agricultural paradise—which is how the Canadian Pacific Railroad advertised it in the 1890s. For most people, there's wilderness enough five miles up the dirt road the oil industry built along Scarpe Creek, where you can fish for trout with your cooler of Molsons within arm's reach on the seat of your all-terrain vehicle. Rural Canada has fallen head over heels for the ATV or "quad" as it's known in these parts. The machines can tackle the most primitive oil and logging tracks. They make their own trails, dispersing wildlife, despoiling habitat, fouling streams. They aren't supposed to be in the Castle-Crown Wilderness, but people ignore the regulations. From the traffic and the noise, you'd think most of Calgary was motoring around the forest roads on a summer week end. We find a pair of quads parked outside the one-room cabin Mike built for hunting clients. The two teenage drivers are fast asleep in side. Mike rousts them with a sharp knock and a stern warning about the penalty for trespassing. He won't press charges. He can't take the risk. His isolated camp is too vulnerable to reprisal. He asks the boys if they are familiar with the signs prohibiting ATVs in the back country.

"Them yellow ones?" one of the boys answers distractedly. "Yeah, my dad is on the committee that drew up the rules."

They board their machines and sputter off. Mike goes looking for his horses.

We ride two and pack six. I bring up the rear on a stout Appaloosa named Traveler, and it's my job to make sure no one turns tail and heads for home. Mike doesn't believe in keeping his horses roped, one behind the other. A conventional pack train would become hopelessly snarled in the forest, especially on the bushwhacker's route Mike prefers to better-traveled trails. We thread our way through dense stands of lodgepole and larch, the packhorses maneuvering expertly, their cargo of wooden grub boxes barely brushing a tree trunk. I'm not so agile. Before I know it, both sleeves of my shirt are shredded. My hat is gone and my forehead bleeding. "What's keeping you?" Mike asks, only half in jest, when I catch up with him. "I thought you said you could ride a horse." He points to the ground, where a pile of bear shit glistens in the afternoon sun. "The old man of the mountain has been here and not that long ago. Good sign."

The pine trees give way to a jungle of shoulder-high huckleberry and lacey white bear parsnip. At one point we are surrounded by water like a bayou—Louisiana in the Canadian Rockies. The packhorses spread out in all directions, snacking on green clumps that float like hyacinth. Mike is out of sight, and I am no longer sure which way he is headed. I push on, down a watery aisle of giant, swaybacked cottonwoods, taking my cue from Traveler, who seems in no particular hurry, clip-clopping through the shallows. I am not worried about getting lost. That would take work in a place where every canyon defaults to a road. Besides, the point of wilderness is not so much to get lost as it is to lose yourself, to be immersed in the ecology of Genesis, the world before the Fall. Or so it seems to me as I stare down at the red and green pebbles of argillite—compressed sandstone, baubles from the Pleistocene—that form a shimmering, tiled avenue through the cottonwood.

"There's no good argument for wilderness," Mike says that evening after supper. "There simply isn't one. If there were, we'd be winning. I've spent the better part of my life arguing for it and having no success. We can't even keep a little band of wolves alive in these mountains. The ranchers shoot them on sight. You'd think people would want to keep a bit of this wild country preserved. It's part of their heritage. But they're afraid of it. They think progress will cease, and they will be back living in dugouts on the prairie like their great -grandparents."

It's an enduring preoccupation, part fear, part fascination. How else explain the perennial popularity of movies from *King Kong* to *Jurassic Park* that conjure worlds where the apes and dinosaurs are back in charge? Thomas Cole, the first American artist to glorify American wilderness, warned against trying to destroy it. In the *Course of Empire,* painted in 1836, Cole presented a sequence of four tableaux in which civilization transforms wilderness in one scene, only to succumb to it in the last. Cole's point was that as society turned its back on its wild origins, it lost the strength and vigor needed to sustain itself. Yet, Cole himself was uneasy in the wilderness. "The sublime features of nature are too severe for a lone man to look upon and be happy," he wrote in his journal. Cole captured

America's ambivalence toward wilderness in his painting *The Oxbow.* On one side is a scene of rugged, storm-lashed mountainside. On the other side, across a meandering river, is a serene, sunny rendering of farms and fields. I had stood at such a divide often enough in the past two years, avoiding judgment, acknowledging the allure of both places, granting the cowboy his due while ruing the damage he has done to the wilds. But you can get a little too comfortable occupying a neutral vantage point. Sitting by a campfire in Canada, I recall the Texas political adage about what you find in the middle of the road: yellow stripes and dead armadillos.

It takes an ex-cowboy like Mike Judd, himself a weekend painter, to distinguish between art and life. In actuality, the two sides of Cole's famous canvas do not abide peacefully and never have. The Continental Divide north of the U.S. border to Banff National Park is no different. On the map, it is a 200-mile long ribbon of green denoting protection, that bulges expansively as it passes through areas like the Castle-Crown Wilderness, Crowsnest Provincial Park, Kananaskis Country and the Elbow Sheep Wildland. In actuality, much of that land is open to real estate development, roads, ski re sorts, dams, mines, logging, off-road vehicles, and, of course, oil and gas. Mike made his position clear sixteen years ago when he blocked a line of Shell Canada bulldozers in the process of gouging a road to the 7,000-foot summit of Corner Mountain. There the company planned to sink gas wells in the middle of some of the best remaining bighorn sheep habitat in southern Alberta. The area had been designated a "Prime Protection Zone" for wildlife, making it illegal to tear up the ground without a permit from the chief forester for the region. Mike believed that if he could hold off the bulldozers, his friends in the Alberta Wilderness Association could secure an injunction barring Shell's intrusion. He was wrong. After a brief standoff, someone from the oil company produced a permit from the chief forester's office, clearing the way for the bulldozers. A constable who had been summoned to the confrontation was a neighbor. He put his arm around

Mike and tried to comfort him. "I know how you feel . . ." But Mike would have nothing of it, according to author Sid Marty, who was also there and who described the scene in his book, *Leaning on the Wind.* "It's greed," he yelled. "After all the bullshit, it gets down to one thing: just greed."

Mike quit the Alberta Wilderness Association. Of its 2,500 members, four had shown up to lend support on Corner Mountain. Later, he resigned from another environmental group, the Castle-Crown Wilderness Coalition, accusing the leaders of terminal timidity. He grew testy and aloof. Friends feared he was spoiling for a fight he couldn't win. Mike's homestead in the Screwdriver Valley is surrounded by gas wells, pipelines, and relay stations. There are six sour gas wells within two miles of his house. Sour gas is so named because it contains hydrogen sulfide. The gas that comes out of Screwdriver Valley is rank with H_2S. You can taste the sulfur in the tap water. Up close, a whiff of sour gas can kill you. A fatal dose is undetectable because it deadens the sense of smell. A concentration of .06 of 1 percent or 600 parts per million is lethal. One part per million can cause spontaneous abortions. People who had known Mike for a long time worried about the neurotoxic effects of living around sour gas. They wondered aloud if chronic exposure was the cause of his bursts of anger and his curt dismissals of old friends.

Mike has a different explanation for his conduct. "Nobody wants to be perceived as not being nice. I guess I got over caring about that when I watched the bulldozers tear up Corner Mountain. It was the most beautiful place in the world. When I saw them go up there, I knew they'd go anywhere for a cup of gas."

In 1997 one of Mike's neighbors found a dead cow and calf near a gas line. Shell investigated and found a perforated pipe and a leak. During the next two years, they found forty more leaks. Mike and his neighbors argued that the network of lines that crossed their land was rotten with corrosion and should be shut down. The Alberta Energy and Utilities Board eventually ordered Shell to move part of the system, a junction where five pipelines came together, and faulted the company for being unresponsive to the fears of local residents. The board gave Shell two years to relocate. In the summer of 2000, with the pipeline junction still in place, the company began work on another well near Mike's property. "It was a pretty tense summer. At the end of it, my girlfriend moved out. I couldn't blame her. She had two kids and this was no place to raise them. It was around that time I took things into my own hands, you might say."

He "borrowed" his cousin's Caterpillar and started driving toward the South Castle River, where a road was being punched into the wilderness to provide access to the newest well site. "Being a little bit drunk, I wasn't exactly sure what I was going to do, just something to stop the bastards." His cousin and the police found him parked at the head of the road and coaxed him down. "They said I was depressed and needed to be hospitalized. That's when they put me in the county unit in Lethbridge. They kept me there for three weeks. The nurses could see I wasn't crazy. They asked me what I was doing there. I said I was a political prisoner."

We stop the first night in Calamity Basin and set up camp across a teardrop lake from an amphitheater of sandstone that soars 1,000 feet, straight up to the Continental Divide. We sit outside our tents, swatting mosquitoes, waiting for the long July twilight to drain the heat from a hot, tired day.

"So what are the colors you see in that rock?" Mike asks, nodding at the cliff wall. "Do you see purple?"

"It's gray."

"I would paint it purple."

The wall is so close and so vast, you can only take in a piece of it at a time. Binoculars add dimension but not color. There are niches and apses; side altars and catwalks; soundless waterfalls and tiny land slides that tinkle like wind chimes. Halfway up the cliff, three white specks, mountain goats, forage on a fringe of green.

We see what we see. John Muir compared the Sierra Nevada to a cathedral. James Watt, President Reagan's Interior Secretary, pronounced the Grand Canyon a bore.

The rock is purple. The air smells like gin.

Up here, the Continental Divide becomes the great wall of the imagination, crowned by crumbling domes and turrets as it zigzags its way north and disappears into the clouds. This is the mythic Divide, the one that made conquering heroes of the first explorers to breach it: Escalante, Lewis and Clark, Pike, Carson, Fremont, and the Canadians: Thompson, Palliser, and Blakiston. To the southwest is Kootenay Pass where the Kootenay Indians tried to sneak by the Blackfeet, fierce guardians of the Divide country, to hunt in the game-rich valleys of the east-facing Rockies. Barely visible on the southern horizon is Chief Mountain, the sacred summit of the Blackfeet. Like a long, jagged reef, the Divide remains the last bastion of the ancient world. But we have laid siege to its flanks, like an army of carpenter ants. Roads reach high up the sides from all directions. Loggers' clear cuts have shredded the forest canopy. From up here, the vast sweep of bare ground looks like a fairway for giants.

Industry blights the American side of the Divide, as well. Thousands of oil and gas wells dot the Great Divide Basin. More are contemplated in the heart of grizzly country in the Bridger-Teton National Forest and just outside the Bob Marshall Wilderness in Montana. Acid rain falling over Wyoming's Wind River Range is poisoning the largest herd of bighorn sheep in the Rockies. Cattle still scavenge for sprigs of grass along the butchered tablelands of the Rio Puerco valley in northern New Mexico, an area so overgrazed it has been described as the worst example of desertification in the United States.

Public opinion polls in Alberta say 80 percent to 90 percent of the people want the remaining wilderness preserved. Polls in the United States tend to reflect similar views. So why don't the politicians heed them? Because the politicians don't believe the polls? Because when they watch the television news and see Mike Judd standing virtually alone against the bulldozers on Corner Mountain, they realize his cause lacks a certain force majeure? In the United States public support for wilderness often weakens if people believe that protecting it will cost jobs. That argument is often made; but the truth is there aren't that many jobs left in the wilderness. The national forests have been shorn of much of the oldest and most valuable timber. Technology and automation have steadily reduced employment in the mining and oil and gas industries. Often, the people who lose their livelihoods are the ones who depend on wilderness, outfitters and guides, people like Mike Judd.

"At some point, you come to the conclusion that most of your fellow citizens don't really mind this shit," Mike says, gesturing at the ravaged Kishinena Valley below us.

We reach the top of the Divide the next morning and travel along it for the next several days, moving along a game trail around Kishinena Peak to Kootenay Pass, then doubling back through Waterton Park and over Sage Pass. In a dense fog we follow a route that is more ledge than trail, a misstep from oblivion, along the roof of the Divide. The fog is so thick, I have trouble seeing the horse in front of me. Chalky buttes and hoodoos appear and disappear in the mist. Suddenly, we plunge knee-deep in a terrace of snow. My horse snorts and shudders violently. Ahead, Mike dismounts and examines a set of tracks in the snow. "Grizzly," he says. "And not too far ahead of us."

We skirt a series of low peaks and passes named after obscure British civil servants, Font, Matkin, Jutland, and Scarpe, ending the week in a fragrant meadow called Onion Basin. We pitch camp, eat what there is left to eat, and lie back in the coarse grass against our saddles. A wilderness doesn't always wear an Old Testament scowl. Onion Basin makes me think of A. A. Milne's 100 "Aker" Wood. It is one of those strangely egalitarian places, like a demilitarized zone, where nature feels safe enough to let down its guard. Baby animals wander out of their dens. Elk wallow in the dirt. Here the horses shed their soldierly demeanor as they roll on their backs, bicycle their feet in the air, and nicker quietly.

I go to bed chewing on a comment Mike made several days ago. "There's no good argument for wilderness," he said. But why should we have to justify wilderness? We get pleasure from it. Isn't that enough? Is there a better argument for building more golf courses or buying bigger cars or having more children?

I didn't grow up in the wilds. I'm a product of suburbs who gravitated to cities, the bigger, the better. I discovered wilderness on weekends and vacations, but I never thought of those trips as retreats or escapes. I found wilderness, in its own way, to be as as vibrant and stimulating as a big city. Urbanites are addicted to stimuli, their antennas restlessly probing for some intriguing discovery—be it food, fashion, architecture, knowledge, or experience. We go through life the way a child explores a new house, in search of wonder. It may take us to different places because we don't have the same tastes. Yet, I cannot imagine that if the design of the world were ours to do over that we would leave out wilderness any more than we could conceive of Athens without the Parthenon, Paris without Notre Dame, or New York without the Statue of Liberty.

At one point on this trip, riding across the top of the Rockies, looking down at the roads and the clear cuts and all of the places where civilization was carving its initials, I remembered General Electric's famous slogan. "Progress Is Our Most Important Product." I first heard it in the 1950s on my parents' G.E. television set, which itself was the most visible sign of progress in our house at the time. The words of the commercial were usually accompanied by scenes of a sleekly modern kitchen, its seamless ensemble of built-in cabinets and appliances a stark contrast to our homely assortment of wooden cupboards, freestanding icebox, chipped Formica, and faded linoleum. Today, G.E.'s slogan might well be the mantra of global capitalism, certainly of the industries that are marching up these mountainsides, relentlessly mining the resources and transforming the environment, making it more accessible, more familiar, and safer. But is that what we want, to purge the world of all traces of its ancient unruliness, to wean society off its primal longings and tribal leanings, to alienate the animist and the tree hugger, to tidy up the planet? The roots of our own culture are in wilderness. The stories of our history and the legends of our heroes are entwined with it.

Wilderness is the swamp we drained to build a mall before we understood that swamps absorb our waste water and filter out the toxins. It is the urban forest we cleared away before we learned that its root system held the city's watershed in place. Wilderness is the unquantifiable, unfungible asset, the one the accountants scratch their heads over when they are trying to value the estate. It is a tree lying across the path to the future, a place to pause long enough to remember Thomas Cole's vivid warning about the perils of progress. The headlong rush to the future, Cole suggested, can cut us off not just from nature, but from our better nature. We took this land from people who believed that the mountains were the realm of gods, who came here for divine inspiration. Today, as we watch the grandest buildings disintegrate in fiery clouds, is there not some reawakened impulse for simple sanctuary, for the places that remind us of what God first wrought, of "purple mountains' majesty"?

The grizzly comes in the night. I hear his footfalls, but I don't fully awaken. I remember wondering semiconsciously what large animal would walk so softly. I have been visited by grizzlies before. It is an experience that can leave you babbling to yourself, as if a meteorite has landed in camp. But this bear in this place does not rouse me and I fall back to sleep, as if the whole thing had been an animated dream inspired by Dr. Seuss of pachyderms on tiptoes.

"Did you see the bear?" Mike asks the next morning. "He must have walked right between our tents." Keeper, his dog, had noticed first, bristling and staring at the wall of Mike's tent, but not moving or making a sound. Mike stepped outside. At first, he saw nothing, but as his eyes adjusted to the dark, his gaze was drawn to a large form about fifty feet from the camp. Mike and the bear looked at each other for a long moment. Then the grizzly turned and disappeared into the forest.

We search the ground for tracks, but the grass is thick and we don't find any. Still, the bear has its hooks in us, and we can't quite ignore the temptation to follow unseen footsteps. How long would it take, I ask Mike, to get to the high north, to the country beyond the settlements and the parks and the roads—up there where the bears still number in the thousands? He gets out a map, flattens it out on a stump, and moves his finger slowly up the Divide. We have enough horses and probably enough time. It's early July. We could resupply at Crowsnest Pass and Bow Valley, make it through Banff and Jasper to the Willmore Wilderness by September. It's not the Yukon, Canada's northwestern frontier. But it's the antechamber.

Thunder mumbles in the west, a gentle warning. It is the first sign of the summer storm season and Mike wants to be down in the low country before it arrives. He takes a last wistful look at the map and puts it away. "We'll do it next time," he says. We saddle the horses, load the boxes, and head down a steep, rocky trail, our backs to the Divide.

Author Biographies

Peter Anderson, author of *First Church of the Higher Elevations: Mountains, Prayer, and Presence,* has lived in the American Southwest for over twenty-five years, working as a river guide, journalist, teacher, wilderness ranger, and editor. He is the author of many books on nature and spirit, including several biographies of conservationists written for younger readers. He lives on the western slope of the Sangre de Cristo Mountains in southern Colorado, where he serves as editor of *Pilgrimage* magazine (www.pilgrimagepress.org) and poetry editor for the *Mountain Gazette.*

Caroline Arlen spent two years traveling across the country interviewing miners for her book *Colorado Mining Stories: Hazards, Heroics, and Humor.* Time essayist Roger Rosenblatt had this to say about the finished product: "What great good luck to find a first-rate writer who has found a first-rate subject. In unearthing the stories of Colorado miners, Arlen presents a rich new look at American history through the first-person narrative of an array of tough, brave, strange and fascinating people."

Audrey DeLella Benedict is the founder and director of Cloud Ridge Naturalists (www.cloudridge.org), a nonprofit natural history field study organization. She is also a trustee for the Colorado chapter of The Nature Conservancy and is active in conservation projects in Colorado and South America. Her *Sierra Club Naturalist's Guide to the Southern Rockies* is soon to be published in an updated edition by Fulcrum Books. Her most recent book, *Valley of the Dunes: Great Sand Dunes National Park and Preserve,* blends her words with the images of award-winning photographers Bob Rozinski and Wendy Shattil.

John A. Byers, author of *Built for Speed: A Year in the Life of Pronghorn,* is a professor of zoology at the University of Idaho. In 1998, he won the Wildlife Society's Book of the Year Award for *American Pronghorn: Social Adaptations and the Ghosts of Predators Past,* a book based on his twenty years of field study. He also has a strong interest in the evolutionary origins and adaptive significance of play and edited, with Marc Bekoff, the 1998 book *Animal Play: Evolutionary, Comparative, and Ecological Perspectives.*

SueEllen Campbell, author of *Even Mountains Vanish: Searching for Solace in an Age of Extinction,* is a professor of English at Colorado State University and a fifth-generation Coloradoan. She is the author of an essay collection, *Bringing the Mountain Home,* was a coeditor and contributor to *Comeback Wolves: Western Writers Welcome the Wolf Home,* and is now writing a guide to landscapes in nature and culture.

Douglas Chadwick, author of *True Grizz,* is a wildlife biologist and author of several books of natural history, including *The Fate of the Elephant,* named by the *New York Times Book Review* as a Best Book of the Year, and *A Beast the Color of Winter: The Mountain Goat Observed.* In 2006, Sierra Club Books will publish his latest book, *The Grandest of Lives: Eye to Eye with Whales.* He also serves on the board of Vital Ground (www.vitalground.org), a nonprofit organization that safeguards habitat for grizzlies and other North American wildlife.

Craig Childs, author of *Soul of Nowhere: Traversing Grace in a Rugged Land,* has written several books based on his intimate knowledge of the American outback, including *The Secret Knowledge of Water, Stone Desert: A Naturalist's Exploration of Canyonlands National Park, Crossing Paths: Uncommon Encounters with Animals in the Wild,* and most recently, *The Way Out: A True Story of Ruin and Survival.* In 2002, he received the Spirit of the West Award from the Mountains and Plains Booksellers Association, honoring his growing body of work.

Frank Clifford has been a journalist for more than thirty years and is currently serving as the environmental editor for the *Los Angeles Times*. Before moving to California, he wrote about the American West for newspapers in Santa Fe, Tucson, and Dallas. *The Backbone of the World: A Portrait of the Vanishing West along the Continental Divide* is his first book.

Stanley Crawford, author of *The River in Winter,* has written two previous works of nonfiction, *A Garlic Testament: Seasons on a Small New Mexico Farm,* and *Mayordomo: Chronicle of an Acequia in Northern New Mexico,* which won the Western States Book Award in 1988. He is also the author of five novels, including his most recent, *Petroleum Man,* and the just reprinted *Gascoyne.* For more than thirty years he and his wife Rose Mary have lived and farmed in the Embudo Valley north of Santa Fe.

Gary Ferguson, author of *Hawks Rest: A Season in the Remote Heart of Yellowstone* (winner of a Mountains and Plains Booksellers Award), has written over a dozen books on nature and science, all concerned with the impact of the natural world on our lives. Since the publication of *Hawks Rest,* he has written *The Great Divide: The Rocky Mountains in the American Mind* and *Decade of the Wolf: Returning the Wild to Yellowstone* (coauthored with Douglas W. Smith).

Richard F. Fleck, author of *Breaking through the Clouds,* is a retired dean of arts and humanities at the Community College of Denver. Previously he was a professor of English at the University of Wyoming, where he taught Native American literature and the regional literature of the American West. In addition to his two novels, *Clearing of the Mist* and *Spirit Mound,* he has published several volumes of poetry and a scholarly study of Henry David Thoreau and John Muir. He also is the editor of *A Colorado River Reader.*

Merrill Gilfillan, author of *Rivers and Birds,* has written ten books of poetry and several collections of essays, including *Magpie Rising: Sketches from the Great Plains* and *Burnt House to Paw Paw: Appalachian Notes.* His 1998book *Chokecherry Places: Essays from the High Plains* won both the Western States and the Colorado Book Awards. In 2005, his *Selected Poems 1965–2000* was published.

Andrew Gulliford, author of *Sacred Objects and Sacred Places: Preserving Tribal Traditions,* is a professor of southwest studies and history at Fort Lewis College in Durango, Colorado. His previous books include *America's Country Schools* and *Boomtown Blues,* a history of western towns caught up in the boom and bust of oil shale development. In 2005, he edited *Preserving Western History,* a new collection of writings on public history across the West.

Gillian Klucas, author of *Leadville: The Struggle to Revive an American Town,* is a journalist who has written for *Preservation, On Earth,* and *High Country News,* among other journals. She became so intrigued by Leadville's complex story that she moved there. She now lives in Portland, Oregon.

Jeffrey Lockwood, author of *Grasshopper Dreaming: Reflections on Killing and Loving,*is a professor of natural sciences and humanities at the University of Wyoming. His essays have won a Pushcart Prize and the 2003 John Burroughs Award for Best Essay. He has also written *Prairie Soul: Finding Grace in the Earth beneath My Feet* and *Locust: The Devastating Rise and Mysterious Disappearance of the Insect That Shaped the American Frontier.* In 2006, Skinner House will publish his latest essay collection, *A Guest of the World.*

Dale Lott, author of *American Bison: A Natural History,*was a professor of wildlife, fish and conservation biology at the University of California, Davis. He came naturally to his lifelong interest in bison, having been born on western Montana's National Bison Range, where his grandfather was superintendent. As biologist Harry Greene wrote, "Lott grew up among these creatures . . . and his engaging prose crackles, almost rumbles at times with a deep appreciation for them and their surroundings." Dale Lott died in January 2004.

Laton McCartney, author of *Across the Great Divide: Robert Stuart and the Discovery of the Oregon Trail,* grew up on cattle ranches in Colorado and Wyoming and is a graduate of Yale University. Winner of the Jessie H. Neal National Business Journalism Award, he is also the author of *Friends in High Places: The Bechtel Story.*

Andrea Peacock, author of *Libby, Montana: Asbestos and the Deadly Silence of an American Corporation,* is a journalist who has covered western environmental news since 1991. Her articles have appeared in several publications including *Mother Jones, Amicus Journal,* and *High Country News.* In 2006, Lyons Press will publish her second book, *The Essential Grizzly,* co-authored with her husband Doug Peacock.

Diane Josephy Peavey, author of *Bitterbrush Country: Living on the Edge of the Land,* grew up on the East Coast and spent many summers driving across the West with her father, historian Alvin Josephy, Jr., before she married and moved to a ranch in Idaho. She has served on the board of directors for *High Country News* and is the founder and director of the Trailing of the Sheep Festival, a folklife festival that celebrates the people, traditions, and history of the western sheep industry.

Ann Ronald, author of *Ghost West: Reflections Past and Present,* is a professor of English at the University of Nevada, Reno. Among her many books are *Earthtones: A Nevada Album* (with photographer Stephen Trimble), *The New West of Edward Abbey, Words for the Wild,* and her most recent *Readers of the Purple Sage: Essays on Western Writers and Environmental Literature.*

George Sibley, author of *Dragons in Paradise: On the Edge between Civilization and Sanity,* is a professor at Western State College in Gunnison, Colorado. He publishes frequently in *High Country News,* the *Mountain Gazette,* and *Colorado Central.* He was briefly a newspaper publisher in Crested Butte in the 1960s. His first book, *Part of a Winter: A Memory More Like a Dream,* chronicled the winter his family spent in Colorado's Gothic Valley, where they were caretakers for the Rocky Mountain Biological Laboratory.

Stewart L. Udall, author of *The Forgotten Founders: Rethinking the History of the Old West,* was elected to four terms as congressman from Arizona before being appointed by John F. Kennedy to serve as Secretary of the Interior, a position he held until the end of the Johnson administration. A member of one of the West's most prominent families, he is the author of many books, including *The Quiet Crisis, The Myths of August: A Personal Exploration of Our Tragic Cold War Affair with the Atom,* and *Majestic Journey: Coronado's Inland Empire.*

Chip Ward, author of *Hope's Horizon: Three Visions for Healing the American Land,*is a writer and activist in service to both land and community. He sits on the board of the Southern Utah Wilderness Alliance and is the author of *Canaries on the Rim: Living Downwind in the West,* an account of grassroots organizing and citizen activism.

Mary Taylor Young, author of *Land of Grass and Sky: A Naturalist's Prairie Journey,* is a writer, biologist and naturalist. She is the author of several books including *Watchable Birds of the Rocky Mountains, Colorado Wildlife Viewing Guide,* and *The Guide to Colorado Birds.*

Ann Zwinger, author of *Beyond the Aspen Grove,* has written over a dozen books, including *Run, River, Run* (winner of the John Burroughs Medal), *Downcanyon* (winner of the Western States Book Award), and *The Mysterious Lands: The Four Deserts of the United States.* She has been honored with the Orion Society's John Hay Award and the Mountains and Plains Booksellers Spirit of the West Literary Achievement Award for her long career of writing about western lands.

Permissions

"Trail Notes—Four Corners—1986" from *First Church of the Higher Elevations: Mountains, Prayer, and Presence* by Peter Anderson. Copyright 2005. Reprinted by permission of Ghost Road Press.

"Mabel Lyke, Grand Junction, Colorado" from *Colorado Mining Stories: Hazards, Heroics, and Humor* by Caroline Arlen. Copyright 2002. Reprinted by permission of Western Reflections Publishing.

"Spring Ritual" from *Valley of the Dunes: Great Sand Dunes National Park and Preserve* by Audrey DeLella Benedict. Copyright 2005. Reprinted by permission of Fulcrum Publishing.

"Grassland Calculus" from *Built for Speed: A Year in the Life of Pronghorn* by John A. Byers. Copyright 2003 by the President and Fellows of Harvard College. Reprinted by permission of Harvard University Press.

"The Voice of the Crane" from *Even Mountains Vanish: Searching for Solace in an Age of Extinction* by SueEllen Campbell. Copyright 2003. Reprinted by permission of the University of Utah Press.

"Real Bear Clawing the Backbone of the World" from *True Grizz* by Douglas Chadwick. Copyright 2003. Reprinted by permission of Sierra Club Books.

"Snake Calendar" from *Soul of Nowhere: Traversing Grace in a Rugged Land* by Craig Childs. Copyright 2002. Reprinted by permission of Sasquatch Books.

"Oh, Canada" from *The Backbone of the World: A Portrait of the Vanishing West along the Continental Divide* by Frank Clifford. Copyright 2002. Reprinted by permission of Broadway Books, a division of Random House, Inc.

"Reflections in Mud" from *The River in Winter: New and Selected Essays* by Stanley Crawford. Copyright 2003. Reprinted by permission of the University of New Mexico Press.

"Backcountry Ranger" from *Hawks Rest: A Season in the Remote Heart of Yellowstone* by Gary Ferguson. Copyright 2003. Reprinted by permission of the National Geographic Society.

"Solace of Dinosaur Ridge" from *Breaking Through the Clouds* by Richard E Fleck. Copyright 2004. Reprinted by permission of Pruett Publishing.

"Sun Dance Notes" from *Rivers and Birds* by Merrill Gilfillan. Copyright 2003. Reprinted by permission of Johnson Books, a Big Earth Publishing company.

"Ute Trail, Colorado" from *Sacred Objects and Sacred Places: Preserving Tribal Traditions* by Andrew Gulliford. Copyright 2000. Reprinted by permission of the University Press of Colorado.

"Living Downstream" from *Leadville: The Struggle to Revive an American Town* by Gillian Klucas. Copyright 2004. Reprinted by permission of Island Press.

"Good for Nothing" from *Grasshopper Dreaming: Reflections on Killing and Loving* by Jeffrey Lockwood. Copyright 2002. Reprinted by permission of Skinner House and the Unitarian Universalist Association of Congregations.

"Bison Athletics" from *American Bison: A Natural History* by Dale Lott. Copyright 2002. Reprinted by permission of the University of California Press.

"Foreword" from *Across the Great Divide: Robert Stuart and the Discovery of the Oregon Trail* by Laton McCartney. Copyright 2003. Reprinted by permission of Free Press, a division of Simon & Schuster.

"Alley's Miracle Ore" from *Libby, Montana: Asbestos and the Deadly Silence of an American Corporation* by Andrea Peacock. Copyright 2003. Reprinted by permission of Johnson Books, a Big Earth Publishing company.

"Life on the Ranch" from *Bitterbrush Country: Living on the Edge of the Land* by Diane Josephy Peavey. Copyright 2001. Reprinted by permission of Fulcrum Publishing.

"Savage Basins" from *GhostWest: Reflections Past and Present* by Ann Ronald. Copyright 2002. Reprinted by permission of the University of Oklahoma Press.

"Sawmill" from *Dragons in Paradise: On the Edge between Civilization and Sanity* by George Sibley. Copyright 2004. Reprinted by permission of Mountain Gazette Publishing.

"The Wild West Masquerade" from *The Forgotten Founders: Rethinking the History of the Old West* by Stewart L. Udall. Copyright 2002. Reprinted by permission of Island Press.

"I Used to Stomp on Grasshoppers" from *Hope's Horizon: Three Visions for Healing the American Land* by Chip Ward. Copyright 2004. Reprinted by permission of Island Press.

"Tumbleweeds" from *Land of Grass and Sky: A Naturalist's Prairie Journey* by Mary Taylor Young. Copyright 2002. Reprinted by permission of Westcliffe Publishers.

"Preface" from *Beyond the Aspen Grove* by Ann Zwinger. Copyright 2002. Reprinted by permission of Johnson Books, a Big Earth Publishing company.

ROCKY MOUNTAIN 🪨 LAND LIBRARY

The Rocky Mountain Land Library's mission is to encourage a greater awareness of the land. Our 15,000 volume natural history library is especially focused on the land and communities of the Rocky Mountains. The subject range of this collection is both broad and deep, with hundreds of natural history studies of flora and fauna, and many more titles on ecology, conservation, astronomy, geology, paleontology, literature, poetry, Native American studies, and western regional history. Many titles address western land issues, while many concern the various cultures, both ancient and modern, that have inhabited our region.

The Land Library is currently engaged in a site search to provide both the shelves and proper environment for a unique residential land-study center for the Southern Rockies. While our search continues, we are also involved in several outreach programs: the Rocky Mountain Land Series at Denver's Tattered Cover Book Store, Conversations on the Land at Colorado State University, Authors & Naturalists in the Classroom at various schools along the Front Range, the Salida Residency Program (a two-week land-study fellowship in Salida, Colorado), and our new publishing program focused on land and community in the American West.

The Rocky Mountain Land Library exists to extend everyone's knowledge of the land—waking us to the sheer miracle of life on earth, while providing access to the stewardship tools we all need. The Land Library's resources and programs are designed to meet the needs of local residents as well as far-flung visitors (naturalists, researchers, writers, and artists, among others).

For more information on the Rocky Mountain Land Library, please visit our website at www.landlibrary.org.

Tattered Cover Book Store

The Tattered Cover is an independent community bookstore that has served Denver's readers for over thirty years, ever since Joyce Meskis first started a small bookshop in the Cherry Creek North district. Today the store offers an extraordinary selection of titles in three metro locations and a free special event nearly every day. In October 2001, the Tattered Cover partnered with the Rocky Mountain Land Library to establish an author series focused on its home region of the Rockies. In its first five years, the Rocky Mountain Land Series has presented over 200 author readings, panel discussions, and workshops for artists and writers.

With lots of cozy spaces and an ample supply of sofas and chairs, the Tattered Cover has always made readers feel at home. With its unwavering commitment to the community, it has become an integral part of the region's cultural life.

For more information, please visit the bookstore's website at www.tatteredcover.com or call 1-800-833-9327.

About the Artist

Evan Cantor is an artist, writer, and musician living in Boulder, Colorado. His scratchboard illustrations have graced the pages of *Wild Earth, High Country News,* and books published by Westcliffe Publishers and the University of Minnesota Press. He regularly contributes his work to environmental causes, including the Southern Utah Wilderness Alliance, the Northwest Earth Institute, and the Southern Rockies Ecosystem Project. In 2002, he taught a Nature Scratchboard Drawing workshop at Denver's Tattered Cover Book Store as part of the Rocky Mountain Land Series.

Evan Cantor's illustrations appear on the following pages:

ii: *Lunch Rocks,* Bison Peak, Lost Creek Wilderness Area, Colo.

xii: *Death Canyon,* Death Canyon Shelf, Grand Teton National Park, Wyo.

1 (2): *Scarp Ridge,* Raggeds Wilderness Area, Colo.

7 (8): *Wheeler Geologic Area,* La Garita Wilderness Area, Colo.

12: *Tombstone Rock,* BLM Public Lands, Utah

18: *Fremont Cottonwood,* Horseshoe Canyon, Canyonlands National Park, Utah

26: *Tall Trees At Watanga,* Watanga Lake, Indian Peaks Wilderness Area, Colo.

35: *Upper St. Vrain,* Indian Peaks Wilderness Area, Colo.

40: *The Indian Peaks,* summit prospect from Mt. Audubon, Indian Peaks Wilderness Area, Colo.

45 (46): *Lake Helene,* Rocky Mountain National Park, Colo.

71: *Maroon Bells,* Maroon Bells—Snowmass Wilderness Area, Colo.

85: *Lake Hungabee,* Opabin Plateau, Yoho National Park, British Columbia

93 (94): *Lake Lefroy,* Ringrose Peak, Yoho National Park, British Columbia

130: *Winter Sentinels,* Walton Mountain, Routt National Forest, Colo.

131 (132): *Libby Lake,* Sugarloaf Mountain and Snowy Range, Medicine Bow National Forest, Wyo.

141: *Big Tree at West Thumb,* West Thumb Geyser Basin, Yellowstone National Park, Wyo.

145: *Death Canyon,* Death Canyon Shelf, Grand Teton National Park, Wyo.

167 (168): *Ogallala Peak,* Rocky Mountain National Park, Colo.